WE DON'T DO WALKING AWAY

RANGERS FC

WE DON'T DO WALKING AWAY

THE INCREDIBLE INSIDE STORY OF
A SEASON IN THE THIRD DIVISION

Lisa Gray

BLACK & WHITE PUBLISHING

First published 2013
by Black & White Publishing Ltd
29 Ocean Drive, Edinburgh EH6 6JL

1 3 5 7 9 10 8 6 4 2   13 14 15 16

ISBN: 978 1 84502 635 6

Typeset by RefineCatch Ltd, Bungay, Suffolk
Printed and bound by Nørhaven, Denmark

For my family –
Mum and Dad, Scott and Alison,
and Ben, Sam and Cody.

CONTENTS

	Acknowledgements	viii
	Introduction	ix
JULY	Brechin and Entering the Ramsdens Cup	1
AUGUST	Get Out of Jail Card	11
SEPTEMBER	When Harry Met Ally	37
OCTOBER	Something Borrowed, Something Blue	69
NOVEMBER	Elgin Lose Their Marbles	89
DECEMBER	What's the Hampden Roar?	106
JANUARY	Conference Call	134
FEBRUARY	Prime Minister's Question	152
MARCH	Mission: Accomplished	178
APRIL	Green and Whyte and Grey Areas	209
MAY	We Are the People	237

ACKNOWLEDGEMENTS

A big thank you to all the people who agreed to be interviewed for this book, particularly the Rangers manager, Ally McCoist. Thanks also to Carol Patton and Stephen Kerr in the Rangers Press Office and Director of Communications James Traynor, for their help. It was very much appreciated.

To friends and colleagues within the media industry who provided help, advice and guidance (and lifts!) along the way – thank you, you know who you are. I am also grateful to the Press Association for granting permission to work on this project and to the PA's Scottish Sports Editor, Gavin McCafferty, for helping me proofread a massive bundle of pages. Any mistakes, I'm blaming you . . .

Thanks to everyone at Black & White Publishing for their efforts, especially Campbell Brown, for giving the book the green light, and Kristen Susienka, for all her hard work.

Finally, thanks to my family for their constant love and support.

INTRODUCTION

In the summer of 2005, I was handed what many football fans might regard as a dream job: the role of Rangers correspondent for the UK and Ireland's national news agency. I had already worked for the Press Association for five years by then, covering everything from lower division team news to SPL matches and the occasional Old Firm game or press conference if one of the more senior reporters was on a day off or on holiday. I was the leg man (or woman!) for my then colleague Jon West, when Rangers clinched the title in extraordinary circumstances at Easter Road on a day that would go down in history as "Helicopter Sunday". Weeks later, Jon announced his departure from the company and the Rangers gig was mine.

My first assignment was a pre-season trip to Canada. Eleven days in the blistering heat of a Toronto summer, conducting interviews with boss Alex McLeish and players such as Nacho Novo, Barry Ferguson and Fernando Ricksen. For myself, it felt a long, long way from the days spent as a rookie reporter covering lower league games at the likes of Albion Rovers and Dumbarton on a freelance basis for the *Daily Record* and, subsequently, the *Scottish Mirror*. Sure enough, Old Firm derbies and title wins and Champions League nights – home and away – followed, with the highlight undoubtedly the UEFA Cup Final in Manchester in May 2008.

Then, in February 2012, everything changed.

Sure, there had been whispers about administration for months, years even, but no one ever really believed it could actually happen. After all, this was Rangers, holders of a world record 54 titles, a club who had famously delivered "Nine in a Row". European Cup Winners' Cup winners, UEFA Cup finalists. A British institution. On Valentine's Day, the financial collapse of the Glasgow giants was confirmed. The reality of the situation hit home like a Mitre Delta square in the face. In the end, it came down to a race between owner Craig Whyte and Her Majesty's Revenue and Customs to see who could appoint their own choice of administrators first. Whyte won and Duff & Phelps seized control of the club.

The football ramifications, as well as the financial ones, were brutal and swift. Rangers were immediately docked ten points by the Scottish Premier League, leaving rivals Celtic with an unassailable 14-point cushion at the summit. The title race was effectively over. The long battle for survival had begun and challenging their Old Firm rivals for honours would quickly become the least of Rangers' problems.

Before Ally McCoist, great managers had inspired with words as well as trophies. Bill Struth's defiant declaration, "Let others come after us, we welcome the chase" and Jock Wallace's rousing rallying call, "We've got the battle fever on" were as much a part of the fabric of the club as the famous marble staircase inside Ibrox. Two days after Rangers were forced into administration, McCoist produced a one-liner of his own that would perfectly capture the mood of the support and become the unofficial slogan for the fight ahead.

When asked if he planned to quit the job as a result of the financial collapse, McCoist replied, "This is my club, the same as it is for thousands and thousands of Rangers supporters." Then, five words that would send cyber space into meltdown within minutes: "We don't do walking away."

In the weeks that followed, there were claims and counter-claims. There were investigations, inquiries and then more investigations. Whyte gave the impression the so-called "Big Tax Case" was the reason behind the club's insolvency, despite no verdict as yet from the First Tier Tax Tribunal, with Rangers disputing a claim by HMRC that the club's use of Employee Benefit Trusts (EBTs) during Sir David Murray's stewardship breached tax laws. Whyte claimed the potential tax bill could be as much as £75 million. In fact, the real reason he was forced to call in the administrators was an unpaid tax bill he had himself accrued since purchasing Murray's majority shareholding for one pound in May 2011. It also emerged Whyte had used cash from a deal with finance firm Ticketus – eventually worth in the region of £26 million for the sale of future season tickets – to complete his takeover.

Failure to secure an agreement with creditors that would allow the club to emerge from administration resulted in Rangers being consigned to liquidation. Within days, Charles Green's consortium completed the purchase of the business and assets of the club for £5.5 million.

On July 4, Scottish Premier League clubs rejected 'newco' Rangers' application for entry to the top flight after five hours of talks at Hampden. The news would have been more shocking had the majority not already gone public with their plans to vote against the bid after canvassing their own fans and citing "sporting integrity" as the driving factor behind their decision. Only Kilmarnock opted against a 'no' vote, abstaining from the voting process.

The supporters wanted a fresh start in the fourth tier of Scottish football and their wish was granted. Scottish Football League clubs voted 'yes' to Rangers but 'no' to a soft landing in the First Division, and life in the Third Division beckoned. A twelve-month transfer embargo for bringing the game into disrepute under the old regime, successfully challenged in the Court of Session, was reluctantly accepted, along with an agreement to settle all of the old company's football debts. Conditional SFA membership was granted less than forty-eight hours before the start of the new season.

McCoist stated, "It is now over five months since Rangers went into administration. It is time to start playing football again."

It certainly was. As they might say on American reality TV shows, it was the beginning of a journey. A mad adventure that would take Rangers from Annan to Elgin and everywhere in between. And I was going along for the ride.

This book is the story of what happened next.

JULY

Brechin and Entering the Ramsdens Cup

Inside Glebe Park hangs an old framed cartoon from the last time Rangers faced Brechin City. The black-and-white sketch, now slightly discoloured by the passing years, had been carefully snipped from a newspaper more than a decade earlier after the two sides were drawn together in the Scottish Cup. It shows Ronald de Boer, Tore André Flo and Lorenzo Amoruso studying a map of Scotland, looking baffled, as the Italian defender asks, "They call it a city, so where is this Brechin?"

For Brechin, the drawing represents a major occasion in the club's history, a lucrative trip to Ibrox for a third-round tie in front of thousands of people against Dick Advocaat's household names in 2001. For Rangers, it represents the big money, big spending era, when the club's finances were spiralling out of control as Sir David Murray chased success at any cost. Flo, the £12 million signing, whose arrival from Chelsea smashed the Scottish transfer record, was the poster boy for the blank-cheque era. Celtic had previously spent £6 million on Chris Sutton and Murray wasn't joking when he famously boasted, "For every five pounds Celtic spend, we will spend ten."

This time around, the differences in fortunes quite literally could not have been more stark. As my young nephew put it: "What the hell is the Ramsdens Cup and what the hell are Rangers doing in it?" I explained to him that the cup was for Scottish Football League clubs, providing them with a decent chance to win silverware. Rangers were now one of those clubs. The Ramsdens Cup was a competition that wasn't even on the radar a few months earlier; now it was set to provide a monumental moment in the club's history – the first match since liquidation was confirmed, since a new company was formed and since Rangers were dumped in the basement of Scottish football. First Division runners-up Dundee were set to become the Scottish Premier League's "Club 12" and fill the void left by the Light Blues in the top flight. And, as a straight replacement for the Dark Blues in the cup competition, that meant Rangers would face Brechin in the first round after the two clubs had been paired together in the north-east draw.

"Amoruso" actually had a point, to an extent. Despite the football club's name, Brechin's city status isn't officially recognised in the modern era. With a population of around 7,000 it is, according to the match-day programme *A View From the Hedge*, "smaller than the average Glasgow council estate". And probably a lot safer at night. The Angus town has a cathedral, but no train station. The second of those facts was not particularly good news for a non-driver like myself, who did not have the luxury of jumping on a supporters' bus with a carry-out for the journey. Determined to hold on to whatever enthusiasm I could muster so early on a Sunday morning, I set off on July 29 armed with a return train ticket to Montrose, where the number 30 bus would hopefully take me the remaining eight miles to my destination.

Landing in Brechin was a bit like stepping back in time to four years earlier and the UEFA Cup Final in Manchester, only on a much smaller scale. Some claim as many as 250,000 descended on the English city in May 2008. There was clearly no chance of cramming a similar number of bodies into this tiny town, but the similarities were definitely there all the same – the sun was shining and everywhere you looked punters were draped in the red, white and blue of their team, fuelled by a sense of adventure and cheap lager, as bemused locals looked on. More than anything, there was the sense that we were all about to witness something a bit special, one of those days where you would look back in years to come and say, "I was there."

The directions from the driver were simple enough after departing the bus in a residential area: turn right, go straight ahead, through the roundabout, and you'll see the ground a few minutes up ahead. And there it was, the sign pointing to Glebe Park, the home of Brechin City Football Club. Not to be confused with Glebe Street, which is the home of *Sunday Post* favourites The

Broons. The ground has an old-style creaking Main Stand, plus the rather fancy new Trinity Road Stand and a covered terrace with the morbid moniker "the Cemetery End". Best of all, it has a hedge. Yes, that's right, apparently the Glebe is the only ground in Europe to have a hedge, and the impressive beech foliage was even given a trim for the occasion in order to look its best for the television cameras.

The record attendance at the ground was for a match against Aberdeen in 1973, which attracted 8,122 fans. In the modern day, a crowd of 4,123 for the visit of Rangers was as much as club bosses could realistically squeeze into the small venue. Usually there is no segregation in force, except for big cup games, and to describe this encounter as a big cup game was a bit like describing the Empire State Building as quite a tall building. Brechin fans were given red tickets, Rangers fans were given blue tickets. Except there weren't enough blue tickets to go around. Hundreds of Gers fans were turned away from the home end, with Glaswegian accents giving some away, while others failed to pass themselves off as locals by cunningly turning their Rangers jerseys inside out.

For those without a coveted brief, there was the consolation of being able to watch the action live on big screens in pubs around the town, with the added bonus of being able to enjoy a refreshment or two while taking in the game. One boozer even gave away free grub to anyone wearing red, white and blue which was, happily, both teams' colours. Most couldn't understand a word of the Gaelic commentary provided by the BBC Alba coverage but, by the end of the day, one fan had tweeted a pic of the Rangers crest with the words "Sinne Na Daoine" below. Translation? "We are the people."

As well as the local pubs, the Ashvale chip shop near the ground did a roaring trade, eventually running out of fish suppers. The club shop didn't do too badly either, with everything from programmes to pin badges and even a souvenir mug (yours for a bargain six quid) to mark the event.

The players wore the new retro-style jersey with the big crest, which was an homage to the 1972 team, marking the 40th anniversary of one of the greatest achievements by a Scottish team on the Continental stage. That triumphant win over Dynamo Moscow took place in Barcelona but today's legendary line-up would have to settle for Brechin instead. With no squad numbers in the SFL, there was also a retro feel to the team sheet, with the starting eleven actually numbered 1 to 11, just like the old days.

Among those starting were seven players who had represented their country at full international level – Scots Neil Alexander, Lee McCulloch, Kirk Broadfoot and Lee Wallace, as well as United States skipper Carlos Bocanegra, Romanian defender Dorin Goian and Northern Ireland striker Andy Little. Debutant Ian Black played as a trialist, along with the re-signed Little, as both players could not be registered until the following Friday when full Scottish Football Association membership would be granted upon the formal transfer of 'oldco' Rangers' SPL share to Dundee. Youngsters Kyle Hutton, Barrie McKay and Lewis Macleod were also given a run-out.

"I was out of contract in the summer and able to move on for free if I wanted to," Little told me. "I delayed over the summer, which meant I was unemployed for about nine weeks. Rangers weren't able to sign players at that time because of the whole situation. When the result came that we were going to be in the Third Division, it was a difficult decision for me, to decide whether I wanted to drop down and play at that level. But the reason I signed was that I'd been at the club for six years and I'd been waiting for my chance to get a regular game for the team. I signed because I wanted to make an impact and help the club get back to where they should be."

Ally McCoist might not have been able to fill the bench as far as numbers were concerned, but substitutes Kal Naismith, Robbie Crawford, Darren Cole and Scott Gallacher only just managed to squeeze into the tiny covered concrete dugout, with backroom staff forced to settle for a seat on a bench or an ice-box, at the mercy of the elements. The touchline was so close to the punters you were scared to go for a pie or a pee before half-time in case you obstructed one of the players while they were trying to take a throw-in.

The answer to what will no doubt be a pub quiz question one day was, "Andy Little, four minutes" – the scorer of the first goal of the new Rangers era and the time of the goal. The striker raced onto a neat pass from McCulloch and kept his cool to slot past goalkeeper Michael Andrews, sparking wild celebrations.

"It was a strange one. I didn't have a lot of time to think about it," said Little. "It was only four minutes into the game. It was really sudden and probably took me by surprise. It was only after the game that I realised it was such an important moment for the club. There is the whole argument about 'oldco' and 'newco' but the way I looked at it, it was the goal for the fans. There had been so much uncertainty around the club, so for the fans to get back to celebrating a goal that Rangers Football Club scored, that was the most important thing."

The fans were cheering again when one supporter began a wobbly ascent up a floodlight pylon before removing one of his trainers and using the footwear to conduct the chanting crowd. For him, the match-day experience ended abruptly when he was carted off by coppers for a night in the cells, with a breach-of-the-peace charge as a lasting memento of the occasion. However, the biggest cheer of the day was reserved for the sight of the match ball landing on top of the famous hedge.

After months of turmoil, the Gers fans were determined to have a party – but Brechin and the weather were both about to put a dampener on the festivities. The heavens opened and Andy Jackson levelled for the home side just before half-time, a goal that forced the tie into extra-time. A month earlier, Brechin boss Jim Weir and his assistant Kevin McGowne had completed the Three Peaks Challenge, which saw them climb the highest mountains in Scotland, England and Wales for charity. At that moment, the duo must have felt like they were on the verge of conquering Mount Everest. It wasn't to be, and a 102nd-minute winner from reinvented frontman McCulloch sealed the win, to the relief of a

Rangers side who looked rustier than the Tin Man in *The Wizard of Oz*.

Mark Dingwall, of the Rangers Supporters Trust, admitted he was relieved simply to witness a game of football after a summer of turmoil. He said, "I was sitting on the Rangers Fans Fighting Fund when one discussion we had was about how much it was going to cost to put Ibrox into mothballs for a year, when we thought it was very unlikely that we would even get a licence to play anywhere. So, we went from facing into that abyss to actually being able to play.

"Life moves on and you accept what your lot is. We are delighted that the SFL have given us somewhere to play. In fact, going up to Brechin was probably the best I've felt going to a game in years. It was a fantastic day out, a bit of an adventure, with turnstiles and hedges and all that sort of stuff."

In case anyone still wasn't aware that the circus was well and truly in town for the day, a massive marquee was erected on some spare ground to allow what the PA announcer had described as "a worldwide media presence" to conduct our post-match interviews. Most of the forty or so hacks had travelled from Glasgow or Edinburgh but, to be fair, the *Wall Street Journal* did preview the match.

"Normally we play six pre-season friendlies and we've not really had anything," McCoist pointed out afterwards. "It's a good result for us and a great start. That's all we wanted – just an opportunity to get back playing football. We got that today and we are thankful for that."

McCulloch dismissed any notion that Rangers' big stars might struggle to adapt to their new, less salubrious surroundings, claiming, "I don't think there will be a culture shock this season – we are quite a level-headed dressing room."

Fellow goalscorer Little said, "Four days earlier, I was getting on my bike and running around the park on my own. That's what I had been doing over the summer. So, to go from that to getting off a bus and seeing cameramen and fans and media from all around the world was pretty shocking. It was pretty nervy as well being thrown right back into it. The fans are right on top of you and it was brilliant. It wasn't the best game in the world, with the team not quite being as sharp and ready for the match, but we got the result in the end."

According to the match report on the hosts' website, Brechin had given McCoist's new-era Rangers "the fright of their lives". But the headlines would not be dominated by McCulloch, Little, Jackson or even the hedge. The following day's back pages belonged to one man who was quickly proving to be as colourful as his name.

Ibrox Chief Executive Charles Green had claimed in a pre-match interview that "bigotry" was one of the reasons why his club had been denied entry to the SPL. Standing by the side of the pitch and battling to be heard over the tinny tunes from a nearby speaker, Green told a BBC reporter, "Some of it has been driven by bigotry, some of it's been driven by jealousy and some of it's been driven by all the wrong motives."

Celtic's response was to refuse to provide a response,

dismissing the comments as "not worthy of any response". Everything had changed in Scottish football, yet nothing had changed at all.

Only time would tell if the rainbow which appeared over Glebe Park as the final whistle sounded would come to signal a bright new dawn for Rangers after weathering the storm. One thing was for sure, the crock of gold at the end of the rainbow belonged to Brechin City. They might have been losers in a football match, but in financial terms they had as good as won the lottery.

AUGUST

Get Out of Jail Card

AUGUST 7, 2012
RANGERS 4   EAST FIFE 0
Ibrox

At first glance, nothing appeared to be that different. The early evening sun bounced off the impressive red brick Ibrox frontage, as fans milled around Edmiston Drive, making the most of what was left of the mild weather and exchanging score predictions, while the guy flogging the *Number One* fanzine bellowed out the same old sales pitch we had all heard a million times before. Even the sweaty, claustrophobic ten-minute tube ride from St Enoch's underground station had been the same. East Fife were the opponents in the League Cup and there was that usual sense of anticipation that you always get ahead of the first home game of the season. But, like Brechin nine days earlier, this would be no run of the mill cup tie.

For a start, Rangers don't generally feature so early on in the League Cup. In fact, this was their first appearance in the opening round since 1978. To put it into context, that was the year *Superman* was released, Bee Gees disco classic "Night Fever" reached No.1 in the charts and former captain Barry Ferguson was born. Oh, and Scotland thought they were going to win the World Cup in Argentina. Such early round cup ties don't tend to attract bumper crowds on a Tuesday night but the demand for tickets for this clash was so great kick-off was delayed by twenty minutes, with a large number of fans still outside the stadium at 7.45pm.

As well as anticipation, the air was heavy with defiant celebration. Yes, there had been dark days. And, yes, some had even considered the grim possibility that Ibrox had witnessed its last game. But Rangers had endured and the world was going to know about it. Official programme sellers ditched the usual billboards advertising a Lee McCulloch poster or a Lee Wallace exclusive interview in the club's match-day publication. Instead, their kiosks were decorated with scrawled felt-tip declarations that, "Rangers will rise again."

Inside the ground, the voice of an unseen Sandy Jardine boomed out, the words of the Light Blues legend capturing the undivided attention of those quickly filling up the four stands. "Welcome back to Ibrox," he said. "Home of Rangers then, now and forever. After the most difficult period in the club's history, Rangers would like to thank their supporters for not walking away. We are the people."

There was barely a breeze to disturb the corner flags on this night in Govan but no shortage of goose-pimpled flesh. The pre-match entertainment was completed by the dulcet tones of Bob Marley assuring the Ibrox faithful that "every little thing gonna be all right".

Rangers players took to the centre circle to acclaim the supporters ahead of kick-off, and they reciprocated with rapturous applause of their own. Ally McCoist's ranks had been boosted further by a trio of players willing to swap the SPL for the SFL and a place in the Ibrox history books. A League Cup winner with Kilmarnock the previous season, Northern Ireland international Dean Shiels was handed his debut from the start, while strike duo Francisco Sandaza and Kevin Kyle – last seen at St Johnstone and Hearts respectively – were named on the bench. The quartet of new recruits was completed by Emílson Cribari, but the Brazilian had to settle for a seat in the stand as he awaited international clearance. There was no place in the squad for Maurice Edu or Alejandro Bedoya after the American duo expressed a desire to quit the club.

Confirmation also came just hours before the match that former football hardman turned reality TV star Robbie Savage probably wouldn't be signing for Rangers. Not that anyone other than the ex-Wales international thought that he might. The thirty-seven-year-old pundit had offered to come out of retirement the previous month and play for nothing but now conceded that the dramatic move was unlikely to happen. He told his Twitter followers, "Just a quick update on rangers the offer is there and it will remain all season ally has my number and knows if he needs me I'll be there! But it's not going to happen at this moment, they have a good squad for div 3, and don't need an old codger like me!

Lol." Lol indeed. The man who had suffered a broken nose after clattering into a camera while on *Strictly Come Dancing* was officially off the radar. But, more importantly, would Rangers be able to avoid being given a bloody nose of their own against East Fife?

Lee McCulloch required just fifteen minutes to add to his winner at Brechin, collecting a deft pass from Shiels and firing beyond Michael Brown. Had it not been for the heroics of the goalkeeper, the score-line early on would have been much higher. It was hard to tell who was more startled, East Fife by the frantic opening spell or the red fox who made a surprise appearance and bolted the length of the touchline before the onslaught continued. Shiels marked his debut with a goal when he dinked over the goalie after Barrie McKay's shot was blocked. Lee Wallace showed Craig Levein what he was missing when he added to the tally with a fierce drive two minutes after the restart – and twenty-four hours after being left out of the Scotland squad for a friendly against Australia. A clinical finish provided McCulloch with his brace with 62 minutes on the clock, before Sandaza made his entrance with twenty minutes to go and Kyle was handed the final ten.

"It was strange before the game," admitted McCoist. "I was really nervous because I wanted to win the game but I wanted to give the fans something they would be pleased seeing. The eyes of the country have been on us and will continue to be on us this season. We don't want to let anyone down."

Technically, it was a giant-killing, the ruthless disposal of a team from the division above. But the reality in this most surreal of seasons was that a Rangers team packed with internationals had avoided a cup shock on their own patch. It was a tough night for Methil boss and ex-Gers striker Gordon Durie, but the Fifers' impressively named chairman Sid Collumbine could at least take some solace from the fifty-fifty gate money split. Official attendance? 38,160.

AUGUST 11, 2012
PETERHEAD 2   RANGERS 2
Balmoor

Despite such a comprehensive demolition of Second Division opposition, only a fool would assume Rangers would romp their way unchallenged through the forthcoming Division Three campaign. So, naturally, I hot-footed it to the nearest bookie's to snap up odds of 14/1 that they would complete the entire season without dropping a single point. The sudden drop in price suggested I wasn't the only one. Okay, so there would be some awkward venues to visit and some tough games to negotiate along the way, especially during a long, hard Scottish winter. But at least I'd get a decent run for my twenty quid. Wouldn't I?

Peterhead is name-checked in the classic Jules Verne science fiction novel *Journey to the Centre of the Earth* – but it's not at the centre of the earth, it's an Aberdeenshire town that sits at the eastern-most point of mainland Scotland. The Blue Toon was founded by fishermen and remains one of Europe's main fishing ports to this day. It used to have two train stations and now it has none so, in the absence of access to a boat, the best option for me was to secure a lift to the hotly-anticipated SFL3 curtain-raiser with Radio Clyde's Alison Robbie and hope there was enough conversation to last the four-hour drive. The sight of her colleague and ex-Ger Ian McCall making a beeline for the back seat armed with a pillow for the journey suggested he did not feel too optimistic about the banter on offer from either of us.

It was unclear whether the red, white and blue bunting strung around the town was to mark the visit of Rangers or not. But there was no doubt who the "Welcome to Division Three" banner stretched across one of Peterhead's main roundabouts was aimed at. Allegedly the work of Aberdeen fans, the homemade signage was replaced by Union Jack flags as the kick-off time drew closer.

Balmoor officially opened its doors in 1997 after the old Recreation Park ground was sold off to a supermarket chain. A smart stadium with two stands which seat 1,000 fans, the facilities helped Peterhead win their place in the SFL three years later, along with fellow Highland League side Elgin City. The ground's official capacity is 4,000 but the Scottish Cup tie against Celtic in January 2012 attracted a record crowd of 4,505. For those confused by the statistics, the extra numbers were down to temporary terracing being erected, rather than the club selling too many tickets.

The scaffolding was back for the visit of the other half of the Old Firm and, if the rumours are true, was required to pass a "bouncy, bouncy" test carried out by stewards before the gates were thrown open to fans, journalists, Sky Television cameras and curious locals.

Before the players even had a chance to emerge from the changing room, kit man Jimmy Bell was called into action to come up with hastily numbered training tops after both strips Rangers had brought with them were deemed to clash. Perhaps more poignant was the sight of the Irn-Bru SFL badge on the sleeves, replacing the golden SPL Champions arm patches from the previous season.

The departure of a number of first-team regulars over the summer – household names like Allan McGregor, Steven Davis and Steven Naismith – meant McCoist had no real option but to give youth a chance and attempt to mould a handful of experienced campaigners with Murray Park youngsters into a squad capable of delivering the goods. So it was almost fitting, in a season of firsts, that seventeen-year-old Barrie McKay opened the scoring after 26 minutes with Rangers' first goal in their first ever league match outside the top flight, to open his account with his first senior goal for the club. Lewis Macleod's long ball upfield found McCulloch, who nodded down for McKay, and he showed composure and skill beyond his years to finish well.

The first sign that Rangers wouldn't get everything their own way in Peterhead had come a couple of days earlier when they missed out on their first-choice hotel for an overnight stay ahead of the match because the venue had already been booked for a wedding party. The second was Rory McAllister's equaliser, when he skipped past United States captain Carlos Bocanegra and swerved a shot beyond the grasp of Neil Alexander after 64 minutes. The third was the sight of the hosts surging into the lead with nine minutes remaining when failure to clear a corner allowed Scott McLaughlin to pounce and fire home.

Some of the Rangers defending was more criminal than the convicts residing at Her Majesty's pleasure at Peterhead's nearby infamous maximum security prison. But, luckily for McCoist's men, they were about to be handed a get out of jail card on their big day. With only twenty seconds of normal time remaining, a Shiels corner was met by a Kyle header that was diverted on to the crossbar and bundled over the line. The big striker tried to claim the scrappy, last-gasp leveller as his own but the final touch was eventually credited to Andy Little – or, more specifically, his thigh.

"It was a relief more than anything to get the goal," he said. "A defeat would have been a nightmare, a disastrous way to start the league."

Among the sixty or so accredited media were several foreign reporters, including Yann Bouchez from French football magazine *Le Foot*. "In France it was difficult for people to understand that such an important club could be relegated to what would be our fourth division, in an almost amateur championship," he told me. "We thought Rangers were too big to fail and that the Scottish federation would save them from relegation. For a great many French people, Scottish football is just about Rangers and Celtic – they wouldn't even be able to tell you another club's name.

"The game against Peterhead was a fantastic opportunity. To see those hundreds of fans who were used to seeing top games this time against a small team in a very small stadium was surreal. The atmosphere was great. We really could feel the stadium breathing, the emotions. The stadium was very simple but we could see that the organisers were doing their best and they served to the journalists some cakes with beef in them – typically British. Some of the supporters with whom we had travelled by bus left the stadium at half-time to drink a beer; the level of the game was poor and they preferred to drink a pint. But, at the end of the game, most of the Rangers fans were confident."

I asked Yann if he expected Rangers to continue to grow stronger and make a return to the top level of football once again.

"In France we say, 'Great clubs never die,'" he replied. "The thing is, sometimes the resurrection takes a lot of time. It was the case for Reims, in France, who had to wait thirty-three years before coming back to Ligue 1. Concerning Rangers, I think they'll be able to get back to the top level quickly. But I wouldn't try to tell you when they'll be able to fight against Celtic for the Scottish League."

In the same weekend Celtic were in Philadelphia preparing to take on Spanish giants Real Madrid in a glamour friendly, McCoist admitted a tough shift in Peterhead had been "a reality check" for his own side, while his opposite number, Jim McInally, felt a sense of pride and vindication for the basement clubs.

"I hope people respect the Third Division now," said the Blue Toon boss. "We were described as glorified Juniors during the week, and that's disrespectful to the Juniors and to us. The only people who didn't disrespect us were Rangers. I'm proud they're disappointed and proud Rangers won't go through the season without dropping a point – the circus can move on somewhere else now."

What was that about getting a decent run for my money?

AUGUST 18, 2012
RANGERS 5   EAST STIRLING 1
Ibrox

Elsewhere, a campaign dubbed "Sell Out Saturday" had been launched in the hope of attracting capacity crowds to the rest of the matches – especially in the SPL, which was an Old Firm-free zone for the weekend. The mission failed to meet its objective, with the biggest crowd of the day at Pittodrie – for Aberdeen's meeting with Ross County – still 8,000 short of the target. Throw in the Edinburgh derby at Easter Road on the Sunday and the combined attendance for all five SPL matches was 40,383.

A week later, in their maiden Third Division outing at Ibrox, Rangers were determined to show the rest of Scottish football how it was done. East Stirling were officially the worst senior team in the country the season before, finishing bottom of the pile out of all forty-two teams, but they were about to experience one heck of a party. A party with a guest list of 49,118.

"It was quite unbelievable, really," said McCoist. "I looked out of the office at 1.30pm and Edmiston Drive was chock-a-block. It was fantastic. It's a statement and it's really encouraging. When you're getting support like that from the fans, you can only go one way and we must go forward."

Some said the attendance set a new world record for a fourth-tier game of football, although the claim was never properly verified, with suggestions of a bigger crowd at a match in Brazil. Either way, Charles Green was determined to milk the moment for all it was worth when he addressed fans ahead of kick-off. "Never mind 'Sell Out Saturday' – this is 'Sold Out Saturday'," he declared. "That's testament to the passion, loyalty and commitment shown by the Rangers support and we thank you all."

Not content with a state of the nation address, the outspoken Yorkshireman also worked his way through the crowds in the hour or so before the game, pressing the flesh, signing autographs and having photos taken with fans. Like a politician campaigning for office, he just about stopped short of kissing babies, probably only because there was a lack of babies at the match.

You had to hand it to Green. Mere weeks earlier, more than 1,000 fans had staged a protest outside Ibrox over the £5.5 million purchase of the club's business and assets by Green's consortium. Led by former player John Brown, the hour-long demonstration made it clear that the fans did not trust nor want the new owner. Just over a month later, there was still a degree of caution and scepticism about Green's motives, but the relationship between supporters and the new chief executive had definitely thawed. He was met with roars of approval as he continued, "This is just the start of the journey. Let's enjoy the adventure."

The journey hit a roadblock after just three minutes. Someone forgot to tell East Stirling they were supposed to be the kind of party guests who stand at the back of the room minding their own business – not the type who are first up on the dance floor. A shove by Bocanegra on Michael Herd had referee Kevin Clancy pointing to the penalty spot and Paul Quinn did well to keep his composure in a cauldron of noise to convert from twelve yards with an assured effort that comfortably beat Alexander.

If the successful Green charm offensive and the early Shire opener were unlikely, the backing received by Ian Black was simply another eyebrow-raising moment on a day where anything was possible. Three days earlier, the midfielder was jeered by Scotland supporters when he made his international debut against the Socceroos as a late substitute at Easter Road. The unofficial panto villain of Scottish football, it's probably fair to say he was not the most popular figure with the Rangers support either before his switch to Ibrox. Now he was one of their own. As the large banner in the bottom tier of the Broomloan stated: "Welcome to our world, Ian Black. No one likes us, we don't care." There was also a loud cheer when his name was read out before the game, but Black was unable to repay the unexpected affection from the stands with a goal when his long-ranger cracked off the crossbar. The ex-Jambo had to settle for setting up the equaliser instead when he teed up Little to slide past Ryan McWilliams after fifteen minutes.

Little was on target again four minutes before the break when he threw himself in front of a Kirk Broadfoot cross and sent a diving header into the back of the net. Sandaza – handed his first start at the expense of McKay – marked the occasion with his first Rangers goal, stabbing home from close range in a packed goalmouth after attempts from Broadfoot and Dorin Goian were blocked.

By now East Stirling were a spent force, sapped of energy and robbed of the adrenalin rush provided by their impressive start to the game. Little's hat-trick was completed with sixteen minutes to spare when he forced over the line after McWilliams saved well from Sandaza. McCulloch then stroked home in injury-time to claim his fourth goal in as many games.

The Shire players were applauded by all in the stadium as they trudged wearily off the pitch. Goalkeeper McWilliams had been their star performer despite the five goals conceded, but admitted he was bracing himself to face a far tougher audience – his pupils. A classroom assistant at All Saints Primary in Greenock, he was already expecting stick from some of his charges.

"No doubt a few smart ones will come up to me and wave their Rangers scarves or whatever," he said. "But it's good to have a bit of banter with the kids in a classroom setting. We showed we're capable of competing at a good level. To lose five goals isn't the best, of course, but the gaffer was happy with how we acquitted ourselves."

John Coughlin may have been impressed by his side's efforts but the big day was missed by another key figure at the club. Chairman Tony Ford, who suffers from Parkinson's Disease, was unable to attend due to a prior personal engagement but came up with a unique way to ensure his seat in the directors' box at Ibrox would not be empty – by handing one lucky fan the chance to be chairman for the day at one of the club's biggest ever games. Proceeds of an auction, via sealed bids, would be equally shared between the Forth Valley Young Parkinson's Support Group for research into finding a cure and the East Stirlingshire FC Community Engagement Fund for local projects.

Ford explained, "I'm ex-Navy, I worked in submarines, and I had a submariners' reunion down in Crewe. We were actually due to play Stranraer that weekend. When we found out we had Rangers instead, that was rather more of a bad thing for me. I thought, 'What have I done?' I had to accept the fact.

"I suffer from Parkinson's and thought it was an opportunity to get some publicity and a little bit of cash out of it. I put the chairmanship up for auction and there was a lot of good publicity. I asked Rangers if I could do it and they were delighted, they were really accommodating and fantastic, to be fair to them. I had about eight or nine bids and the money varied quite a bit.

"The gentleman who won it was a guy called Charles McLaughlin, who's an old Shire fan. He was absolutely delighted. He used to go to games in the back of a transit van so, this time, he travelled with the team and went to the hotel beforehand and had the full works and met all the players. He's got the bug again and that's what it's all about. It was a really good day for him. He's an enthusiastic guy. I'm delighted that he won.

"The nice thing now is that he's part of my commercial

activities team and he's now helping the club. So, it was probably the best thing I've ever done because, in a way, it's helped us commercially as well. It's been brilliant."

Ford may not have been in Glasgow but was well aware of what was transpiring on the pitch as he took in another football match 240 miles away.

He said, "I had updates. We were at the Crewe versus Notts County game and we were sat in the crowd. I'm a bit of a nervous watcher so I wasn't checking too often. The comment from friends I was with was, 'Bloody hell, you're winning at Ibrox.' It was only about ten past three. We scored about 85 minutes too early but there you go.

"At the end of the day, the trips to Ibrox are not about me, it's not about the club. It's about the players. It's a once in a lifetime experience for some of those guys. We are quite lucky because we've got Queen's Park in our division and play at Hampden every season. That's become a little bit like normality. Some of these players are coming into our team from the Juniors. To play at Ibrox in front of a record attendance, that for a young lad of seventeen years old, who has been playing at one of the Juniors clubs, must have been the absolute thrill of his life."

As far as Rangers were concerned, normal service had been resumed. But surely such comprehensive victories every week would become, well, a bit dull after a while? The question was put to McCoist by a foreign television crew in his post-match briefing. "It won't be boring for me," he insisted. "If you had been at Peterhead last week, it certainly wasn't boring and I didn't find this game boring. We will play tough games, especially away from home, and I can assure you I won't be bored over the next three or four years."

AUGUST 21, 2012
FALKIRK 0   RANGERS 1
Falkirk Stadium

There is nothing boring about winning honours, as a club with a world record 54 titles will testify. And regardless of the level of football now being played, the demands to keep the Ibrox trophy room well stocked were as stringent as ever. The competition sponsor's catchphrase might be "Got gold, get cash," but for Rangers it was all about the silverware as they travelled to the Falkirk Stadium for the second round of the Ramsdens Cup – with a domestic quadruple still a possibility.

Amid all the alien experiences, there was at least a sense of familiarity about this encounter, albeit the memories of the last meeting between the two clubs would not have been particularly comforting for Rangers. As SPL champions, they were unceremoniously dumped out of the League Cup by the First Division side at the same venue the previous September, when a double from striker Farid El Alagui and a late free-kick from former Celtic youth player Mark Millar secured a shock 3–2 win for the hosts over the holders. The result was all the more galling for a Rangers side still basking in the glow of an Old Firm derby triumph just a few days earlier.

This time around, Rangers were determined to turn the tables by inflicting defeat on the team currently in possession of the Ramsdens Cup. There were just three survivors from the League Cup tie – McCulloch, Bocanegra and Alexander. The number would have been four had it not been for the noticeable absence of Goian from the team sheet.

The Romanian defender had established himself as something of a cult figure during his time at the club, even providing the inspiration for the popular #GoianFacts trend on Twitter. Based on the original Chuck Norris jokes, fans took to the Internet to come up with their own "facts" about the centre-half (for example, Dorin Goian created the giraffe by upper-cutting a horse; Superman wears Dorin Goian pyjamas – yup, you get the idea). Unfortunately, the latest #GoianFact was no joke. The fans' favourite was gone, back to Italy on a year-long loan to Serie B side Spezia, just twelve months after his arrival in Glasgow from Palermo.

Goian was replaced in the heart of defence by Cribari, who made his first start after a late substitute appearance against East Stirling, and who brought with him bags of experience from his time in Italy with Lazio, Udinese and Empoli. There was also a full debut for Chris Hegarty, the first player to sign to the 'newco' after his previous contract expired in the summer. The Northern Ireland youngster started at right-back, while Broadfoot shifted to the left to plug the gap left by the injured Wallace. Injury to Shiels also paved the way for a starting role for McKay. The signing of former France Under-20 international Sébastien Faure was confirmed earlier in the day. The ex-Lyon defender, who also had a trial with

Leeds United, was the sixth new signing, subject to international clearance.

Falkirk were now without star man El Alagui, who had departed for Brentford over the summer. Also missing from the match was Dave McIntosh, the stadium's PA announcer, who had been suspended pending an inquiry after allegedly making "inappropriate" comments about Rangers.

The freelance radio broadcaster reportedly referred to the club as "Sevco Franchise" and called Ibrox "Castle Grayskull" while reading out half-time scores during Falkirk's game against Raith Rovers. Sevco Scotland was the name of the company who purchased the business and assets of Rangers before shareholders voted in favour of changing the name to The Rangers Football Club. Castle Grayskull is a fictional fortress in the *Masters of the Universe* cartoon and often used by opposition fans when mockingly referring to Ibrox.

Falkirk chairman Martin Ritchie told his club's website, "It has been brought to our attention that our PA announcer made some inappropriate comments about Rangers at half-time on Saturday. We have already apologised to Rangers FC and would now like to apologise to the many Rangers supporters who have been in contact with the club. Falkirk FC are treating this incident very seriously and the individual concerned has been suspended from his duties, pending a full investigation by the club."

When quizzed about the PA announcer being stripped of his microphone, McCoist said he "couldn't give a monkey's" about the incident, stressing he had "far bigger things to worry about". Top of the list was no doubt ensuring his side's progression in the cup competition.

Bairns boss Steven Pressley claimed beforehand that one Rangers player probably earned more than his entire squad, regardless of their inferior league status. As such, this contest was probably closer than he expected and McCoist would have hoped. The decisive goal came courtesy of Little when he drilled a fine shot past Michael McGovern, picking his spot in the bottom corner on the stroke of half-time. There was also a penalty shout when the ball appeared to hit Chris Smith's hand but no award was forthcoming from referee Calum Murray. For all Falkirk's possession, they lacked the cutting edge in front of goal which saw them triumph the last time.

The positives for Rangers? Their name was now in the hat for the quarter-final draw, Little's hot streak looked set to continue after claiming his sixth goal of the season and Hegarty had delivered an assured performance on his first senior start for the club.

A regular on the bench in the past but yet to make the step up before now, the twenty-year-old confessed, "I found out I was starting two and a half hours before the game and I think that was a good thing for me. I would have been nervous if I'd been told the day before, so it wasn't a bad thing. I felt my performance was solid. The main thing was keeping a clean sheet, and we did that. It was hard but that was the main thing for me."

AUGUST 26, 2012
BERWICK RANGERS 1   RANGERS 1
Shielfield Park

With further progression in the Ramsdens Cup and a last eight meeting with Queen of the South secured, Rangers were about to head even further into uncharted territory. The club had long harboured ambitions of playing league matches in England and now they were about to realise that dream – just not in the way they had hoped or imagined. Berwick Rangers may be based two miles south of the border in the English county of Northumberland, but this clash was light-years away from the promised land of the English Premier League. Little Shielfield Park was hardly Old Trafford or the Emirates, but the town of Berwick-upon-Tweed was bracing itself for a mini Scottish invasion all the same.

A combination of strong coffee and some stunning scenery on the way down through the east coast meant the early morning two-hour train journey over the border was actually very pleasant and civilised. A one and a half mile stroll in the sunshine followed, across the Royal Tweed Bridge into Tweedmouth, where the ground could be found tucked away behind a row of houses.

The Black & Gold social club adjacent to the ground was already proving popular with home and away fans as I made my way into the main stand, where a row of seats was set aside for the written press. Rangers' former director of football Gordon Smith and the rest of the ESPN commentary team had to settle for wooden stools down on the trackside, granting them an unusual vantage point. Directly opposite my seat in the makeshift press box was the east terrace, which included a small covered area in the centre called "The Ducket", and which housed a sell-out travelling support for this match. By day, Shielfield is home to a football club; by night, it hosts the Berwick Bandits. The local speedway team's tenancy meant loads of spare tyres were on show around the ground although, thankfully, not the type caused by too many half-time pies. The nearby Simpsons Malt plant provided an intimidating backdrop to the scene and an excellent view of the action for a few of the workers.

As well as being the only English club to play in Scotland, Berwick boast another football claim to fame that is all too familiar to the Light Blue legions. In 1967 a record crowd of 13,365 watched as the Wee Rangers caused a major upset when they dumped the big Rangers out of the Scottish Cup in the first round. The victory was masterminded by player-manager Jock Wallace, who, of course, would go on to take charge of the Glasgow giants and enjoy a glorious Ibrox reign that included two domestic Trebles in a blistering three-year period.

The mission for the class of 2012 was to ensure they avoided a similar shock to the stars of the '60s, irrespective of the fact that Rangers were visiting Berwick under very different circumstances this time around. Former AEK Athens defender Anestis Argyriou made his debut from the start – sparking mild panic among journalists and broadcasters over the correct spelling and pronunciation of his name – after penning a three-year deal the day before. There was also a first appearance of the season for Ross Perry, who recovered from a calf problem to take his place in the starting line-up.

Youssef Bejaoui did not have a save to make for most of the first half, but the Berwick goalkeeper was plucking the ball out of the back of the net in injury-time. Black's free-kick found McCulloch at the back post and he bulleted a header into the path of the on-form Little to rifle home from six yards. Speaking before the match, self-confessed Rangers fan Fraser McLaren admitted it would mean everything to score against his boyhood heroes. He, too, had experienced first-hand the financial collapse of a football club, sealing his move to Berwick following the demise of Gretna. And you didn't need Mystic Meg to predict what was going to happen next. The home side restored parity after 63 minutes when McLaren dispatched a powerful angled drive beyond Alexander just four minutes after coming off the bench. The substitute could have won the match when he forced a brilliant save from the Gers number 1. Even more unfortunate was Chris Townsley, who had the ball in the net late on, but the effort was mysteriously disallowed by referee Mike Tumilty, denying the Borderers another famous victory.

The last time Rangers crossed the border to play a competitive match on English soil was a Champions League game against Manchester United in September 2010. Like this game, the clash had also ended all square with a share of the points. But the goalless stalemate against Sir Alex Ferguson's side had been a defensive master-class by Walter Smith against one of the most famous clubs in the world, whereas the draw in Berwick was nothing short of unacceptable in McCoist's book.

"That performance was absolutely miles short," fumed the manager, who cast an agitated figure at the mouth of the tunnel as reporters huddled around him. "I cannot tell you how far short that was of what any Rangers supporter or manager or coach would expect from the team. It was just unacceptable. There's a lot of hard work to be done. I'm up for it and, I tell you right now, they will be too because I'll make sure of it. We will go through it and watch it because that was agony. I'll make sure they watch it again."

The result left Rangers fourth in the table, without an away win in Division Three so far. McCoist added, "Brechin was a jolt. Peterhead was a jolt. Falkirk gave us a right good game. I don't know how many jolts we are wanting."

AUGUST 30, 2012
RANGERS 3   FALKIRK 0
Ibrox

Whether McCoist's video nasty did the trick or not would be put to the test when Falkirk came calling for another crack at Rangers, this time in the League Cup. But before attempts could be made to edge closer to a return to the national stadium for on-field matters, there was other Hampden business to be dealt with.

Remember Green's "bigotry" comments? The Gers chief had been asked by the SFA to explain the remarks he made in the interview at Glebe Park and managed to come up with an explanation convincing enough to allow him to escape with a censure. There was also a slap on the wrists for the manager from the governing body, in the form of a twelve-month suspended three-match touchline ban. McCoist was found guilty of bringing the game into disrepute and not acting in the best interests of football – for questioning the independence of the panel that handed Rangers a year-long transfer embargo in April – but would be free to take his place in the dugout for the visit of the Bairns.

The Ibrox exodus continued when Broadfoot reached agreement with the club to be released from his contract, with the narrow victory at the Falkirk Stadium proving to be his last match for Rangers. However, this meeting with the First Division outfit would provide fans with their first opportunity to see new recruit Faure in action, with the Frenchman added to the starting XI, albeit in a holding midfield role rather than his more familiar centre-back position. There was also a double injury boost when Wallace and Shiels both returned from dead legs.

Falkirk fired out a warning in the opening spell when David Weatherston struck the post with a fine right-foot volley that had Alexander well beaten, but the visitors were never able to follow up on their early promise. If the stalemate at Berwick was a slog, this was almost a stroll for the home side in comparison. McCulloch broke the deadlock when he met Black's corner and powered home a header after eighteen minutes. Not to be outdone, Little collected a great pass from fellow countryman Shiels to finish well on 32 minutes. But McCulloch was clearly revelling in the continued opportunity to lead the line and it was he who rounded off a comfortable victory seven minutes after the restart, supplying a composed finish after taking advantage of a horrible defensive mix-up between Smith and goalkeeper McGovern.

With his grey buttoned-up cardigan and brown leather brogues, Falkirk boss Pressley had clearly been taking style tips from his old gaffer Walter Smith, but successful cup nights at Ibrox would be a bit tougher to emulate, and the young manager's side headed back to Westfield smarting from a second cup exit at the hands of Rangers in less than a fortnight.

On the same night his players swept into the third round, McCoist was keeping a keen eye on the fortunes of another Scottish club. Hearts were facing the might of Liverpool in the Europa League play-offs, knowing their chances of advancing to the group stages had all but been written off ahead of the visit to Anfield, having already succumbed to an Andy Webster own-goal in the first leg at Tynecastle. However, a young winger by the name of David Templeton had thrown the Jambos a lifeline when his shot was spilled over the line by José Reina late in the game, briefly providing hope of extra-time before a Luis Suárez strike with two minutes to go allowed the Reds to scrape a 2–1 aggregate win.

Watching his top transfer target perform so well on such a big stage resulted in mixed emotions for McCoist, who confirmed a bid had been tabled for twenty-three-year-old Templeton and now feared the asking price was set to increase. He joked, "I thought it was an own-goal and the goalkeeper probably should have saved it. I would rather anybody had scored that goal, to be quite frank with you, other than David Templeton. All kidding aside, I watched the last fifteen minutes and Hearts were great and it was just really disappointing they lost a goal late on."

McCoist added, "I've said for a number of weeks now that we've got to get bodies in and David is one we would be really keen to get, along with a few others. We have to be busy. I certainly think we need a handful, if not six. What we have to appreciate is that we are an SFL3 team and we have to get out of SFL3 – that's the priority."

Hearts boss John McGlynn made his views on a Rangers swoop crystal clear, saying, "From the manager's point of view, I don't want to lose a player like David Templeton."

A little over twenty-four hours later, David Cooper Templeton was a Rangers player.

SEPTEMBER

When Harry Met Ally

SEPTEMBER 2, 2012
RANGERS 5   ELGIN CITY 1
Ibrox

For those of a certain vintage who were lucky enough to witness the goal first-hand, it is a moment that will never be forgotten. For the rest of us, the grainy black-and-white footage will never quite do it justice but the magic is there for all to see just the same. August 4, 1979. David Templeton was not yet a twinkle in his father's eye, but the man he would be named after gave birth to one of the greatest solo goals ever witnessed in Scottish football. Taking the ball on his chest, with his back to goal, Davie Cooper flicked high in the air four times with that famous left foot of his, past four Celtic defenders in a thrilling game of keepy-uppy, before sliding into the back of the net. The Drybrough Cup Final strike, as Rangers triumphed 3–1 over their great rivals, was later voted the "Greatest Ever Rangers Goal" in a worldwide poll by fans. A story in *The Guardian* hailed the goal as second only to Diego Maradona's "Goal of the Century" in terms of solo efforts. More than anything, it was a snapshot of a career where the word "genius", for once, was not a fawning overstatement.

Simply being given the name of a legend does not guarantee legendary status itself, but a double on your Rangers debut is not a bad way to start. Rangers got their man shortly before midnight on transfer deadline day after a fee reported to be in the region of £800,000 was agreed with Hearts – eight times as much as Jock Wallace paid Clydebank for Cooper's signature in 1977. There are not many players who sign off their career at one club with a European goal at Anfield before beginning life with their new employers in a league match against Elgin City and regard the switch as career advancement. But Templeton appeared more than willing to leave behind the SPL and dive head first into Scotland's basement division. Some, though, questioned his motives and ambition.

Responding to the criticism and the reaction to his move to Rangers, Templeton said, "It was kind of expected, being in the SPL and going to the Third Division. It is a big change and it was something I did really have to think about. But when I came here and saw the facilities and spoke to the gaffer and heard what he was planning for the future, I knew it was a good choice to make. I think once we get back, people will realise that I did make the right choice."

Having spent a couple of seasons at Stenhousemuir, Templeton made the move to Ibrox well prepared for what lay ahead in the lower divisions, adding, "I was used to it, I know what to expect and I know it will be tough. There is a lot that's different and you don't get as much time on the ball. It's something I was used to and learned when I was younger." Hearts also questioned the player's attitude in a parting shot on their website, while praising team-mate Ryan McGowan for snubbing a move to Ibrox and remaining in Gorgie. But, for now, Templeton had enough reasons for making the controversial move. In fact 46,015 of them.

The winger was thrown straight into the action for the visit of the Moray outfit, along with defender Ross Perry, who replaced Carlos Bocanegra on the team sheet. The American centre-half sealed a deadline day move to Racing Santander on a season-long loan, while compatriot Maurice Edu's switch to Stoke was confirmed after weeks of speculation over his future. Rather more low-key than Templeton's arrival was the signing of Australian striker Francesco Stella, who was recruited after a trial period at Murray Park, bringing with him experience from his time in Italy with Chievo and Siena. Two in, two out on the final day of business meant boss Ally McCoist was well short of the numbers he had hoped would swell his ranks. With a twelve-month transfer ban now in place, the window didn't just slam shut, it was boarded up and barricaded for the foreseeable future.

With his first-choice defensive pairing both now out on loan on the Continent, the manager's new look rearguard was woefully exposed early in the game. In the same week glossy '80s US soap *Dallas* was set to make a return to UK screens, even the scriptwriters who came up with Bobby Ewing's return from the dead in the famous shower scene would have deemed this Rangers season simply too far-fetched to commit to paper. For the second game in a row a packed Ibrox was dumbfounded as the home side found themselves a goal in arrears, this time within fifteen minutes of the first whistle.

Failure by the shaky Gers defence to clear a corner allowed Jamie Duff to exchange a one-two with Craig Gunn before the big stopper curled a superb effort into the top corner to hand the small band of away supporters a moment to cherish. Dean Shiels sparked the comeback nine minutes later when he buried the rebound after Lee McCulloch's shot was blocked, paving the way for Templeton to enjoy what the headline writers would no doubt refer to as a "dream debut". He took advantage of fine play from former Hearts team-mate Ian Black to rifle high into the net after half an hour, before McCulloch recorded his 100th career goal on the stroke of half-time. He celebrated by kissing the captain's armband he inherited following Bocanegra's departure, with McCoist describing the decision to promote the utility man to skipper as a "no-brainer". Templeton added to his own tally three minutes into the second half when he turned and drove past John Gibson from close range. There was also a brace for McCulloch, when he happily supplied the simple finish required after Andy Little squared across the face of goal.

McCoist had predicted Templeton would be a crowd pleaser, someone to entertain the Ibrox faithful, and he was not disappointed by his new recruit. "He gives us everything we thought we would get from the wee man," he said. "He takes the ball in tight areas, he commits people and he creates chances and scores goals. In terms of his debut, we couldn't have been happier. He's going to be a real crowd pleaser and I think the fans have already taken to him. It was a good start and I think there is plenty to come from David. As debuts go, you would have to say it was good."

Templeton revealed his frustration at not claiming the match ball on his maiden outing, sighing, "I could have done with one more – I would have liked the hat-trick. I had a few chances but I was still quite tired and I think that showed in the second half and the gaffer took me off. To get the two goals was brilliant, it was a great feeling to score in front of 50,000 and having them all sing my name. It was an unbelievable feeling and I'll never forget it.

"I had spoken to Lee Wallace last season when I was at Hearts and I said that I thought walking out to 'Simply the Best' was unbelievable. But he always said it was better if you walk out and you're on that side. When I walked out this time, I knew what he meant. The atmosphere is so much better when you're playing for Rangers rather than against them. Walking out on the pitch was unbelievable."

Templeton was still a long way away from drawing any real comparisons with the late, great Davie Cooper, but there were enough runs into the box from the left wing and enough clever footwork to provide cause for optimism. But, as was always the case with Cooper, Rangers were quickly learning this was a season where they should expect the unexpected.

Next stop, Armageddon. Or Annan as it's more commonly known.

SEPTEMBER 15, 2012
ANNAN ATHLETIC 0   RANGERS 0
Galabank

Armageddon.

The site of the final battle between the forces of good and evil, according to the Book of Revelation. A 1998 disaster movie starring Bruce Willis and Ben Affleck. And a term bandied about over a summer of discontent whilst predicting the dreadful fate which could befall Scottish football. SPL Chief Executive Neil Doncaster made reference to preventing "financial Armageddon" back in 2010 when discussing plans for league reconstruction, at a time when he was convinced that two ten-team divisions at the top of the senior game was the only way forward. The phrase was widely used again in the summer of 2012 when SFL clubs were asked to vote on whether Rangers should be granted entry into the First Division or the Third Division – with the latter option regarded by some as a doomsday scenario for the game north of the border.

God probably didn't have Galabank in mind as the venue for that epic End of Days battle. But nine games into the season, if the end really was nigh for Scottish football, Annan at least were determined to go out with a bang and a smile on their face. "Annan Athletic's position on the Rangers situation was very clear from day one," chairman Henry McClelland told fans in his programme notes. "Quite simply, we only became members of the league due to the demise of Gretna. Gretna were relegated to Division Three; one season later, Livi received the same fate. To us, it was a clear case of right or wrong. The right thing to do was to put Rangers in Division Three. If it were St Mirren, Killie, etc., there would have been no debate.

"As for Armageddon, we are all loving Armageddon," he added cheerfully. "The interest in tickets has been incredible. I'm sure we could have sold ten thousand tickets to Rangers fans."

A self-confessed Rangers fan himself in his younger days, McClelland – and just about everybody else inside the ground – revelled in the opportunity to meet Light Blues legend McCoist. "The minute I saw him, I got a big cuddle," laughed the Annan chief. "We had never met before but it was absolutely brilliant meeting him and speaking to him. The amount of people Ally took time to speak to . . . The women wanted to have his babies, he is such a personality. Everybody wanted to get their photo taken with Ally and, to his credit, he gave everybody so much time."

Such was the Rangers manager's popularity, his pre-match plans went out the window. McClelland added, "I'd been talking to him at the edge of the tunnel and he was heading back up towards the dressing rooms. I asked him where he was going and he said he was away to do his team talk. I said 'Are you *$%@, you're coming with me!'

"We had 170 people in one of the hospitality rooms, who had paid £100 a head for the hospitality. We've also got a wee bar for our own club members, so I took him in there first and that was a mixture of Annan and Rangers fans and both sets of fans erupted. Then I took him into the big room and they were giving it laldy in there. He acknowledged them all and some of them got photographs. He had been heading to do his team talk and I hijacked him!

"He did the sponsor's draw as well. Because of the limited tickets, you found that a lot of the Rangers fans were buying hospitality packages. So, we had Rangers fans who had paid £100 a head for hospitality just so they could see the game. One of the tables who won the prize were Rangers fans from the Queen Street True Blues and the first prize was a hospitality package for an Annan home game. So there was a wee bit of banter about that as well."

Annan used to be the new boys of the SFL but now looked like veterans next to the latest additions. Founded in 1942, the former East of Scotland League side won admission to the SFL in 2008 after neighbours Gretna went into liquidation. This encounter was set to be one of the biggest matches in their history and the bedsheet brigade were out in force again. Whether the daubed duvet declaring "Welcome to Division 3 from Annan" was a genuine gesture or a cynical dig was open to individual interpretation. But the travelling fans were certainly made to feel at home inside the ground thanks to the PA announcer coming up with a pre-match set-list of tunes that wouldn't be out of place at Ibrox. "Penny Arcade", anyone?

The experience was also memorable for reporters covering the game for different reasons. The press box seats just ten people and, with a main grandstand holding just 500 fans – those who were lucky enough to get their hands on coveted pink tickets for this occasion – Annan were, understandably, determined to cram as many cash-paying punters in as possible. That meant the rest of the journalists were forced to loiter around the side of the pitch, next to the corner flag. Some seats were eventually supplied from the social club but there was still the awkward balancing act of laptop, team sheet, pen and notepad, with the on-field action a little too close for comfort. Television crews also found themselves operating under unusual conditions, with scaffolding erected on the main road outside the ground and shooting of the action taking place through a hole in the fence.

As well as the main stand, the ground has three terraced areas – the Club House End; the East Terrace (where the dugouts are located); and the North End (also known as the Astro End after the AstroTurf training pitch behind it), which usually houses the away fans. Galabank is also one of a handful of Third Division venues with an artificial pitch. The new 3G surface was installed for the start of the current season after the project was funded through grants from Cashback for Communities, sportscotland and Dumfries and Galloway Council.

Five minutes into the match and Templeton must have felt like his own world had come to an end. The winger was in obvious distress as he crumpled to the pitch holding his left ankle, without anyone near him, after running with the ball down the left wing. He was eventually carried off on a stretcher and taken to hospital, adding to a casualty list that already included Little and Anestis Argyriou before the game.

Speaking afterwards, Templeton said, "When I went over on it, it was really sore. But I'd never done my ankle before so I didn't know it was that bad. I was lying down and Lee Wallace was saying to me, 'Try and get up and play on because we need you.' I said to the physio that I wanted to try and he told me to look at my ankle. I looked down and it was like a balloon. That's when I knew it was a bad one. It's really frustrating. I was on such a high – I had just scored at Anfield, I'd got the move that I'd always wanted and I'd scored on my debut. I was flying and for that to happen was gutting."

Templeton's replacement, Francisco Sandaza, was denied by Alex Mitchell after half an hour, when the goalkeeper dived low to save after Shiels fed the Spaniard's run. McCulloch volleyed wide before Jack Steele fired a dangerous, bouncing effort just past the upright for the home side. The midfielder should have opened the scoring early in the second half when he pounced on a loose ball to take him through on goal only to drag wide from fifteen yards.

Neil Alexander's frustration was apparent when he exchanged words with unhappy fans behind his goal, challenging them, "Would any of you like a game?" With no one taking him up on the offer, play raged on. Imposing centre-backs Steven Swinglehurst and Peter Watson were both impressive for Annan, but Rangers were able to carve out a few half-chances before McCulloch failed to snatch the points late on. The skipper caught the ball on the half-volley and seemed certain to find the top corner, until Mitchell threw himself bravely across goal to touch over the crossbar.

The goalless stalemate saw Rangers drop points for a third successive away game in the league, as their search for a victory on the road in Division Three continued. It was hardly Armageddon, but it had been another David and Goliath contest – and Goliath was still coming off second best.

It was a good day all round for the town, who had a memorable result on the pitch to celebrate, while enjoying a bumper payday off it. McClelland said, "The trade the game brought to the town was incredible. One of the hostelries is, without a doubt, the busiest pub in town and the owner has had it for ten years. On September 15, he made the single biggest takings he's ever had in his ten-year history. There was a massive spin-off for the hotels, pubs, clubs and eating places.

"On the Monday morning, the guy who has the pub – it's called The Shed – handed a donation across to us because of the business he got. He said because he had done well that it was only right that the club did well. That was a boost and it was a real bonus that the town benefited as well."

Ally McCoist was clearly frustrated at the full-time whistle, while relief was the overriding emotion for opposite number Harry Cairney, who said, "At some point in their away games, Rangers are going to give somebody a real doing – we are glad it wasn't us." Instead, the man who works as a full-time physics teacher in a high school in Glasgow had given Rangers yet another tough lesson as they continued to adapt to their new surroundings.

SEPTEMBER 18, 2012
RANGERS 2   QUEEN OF THE SOUTH 2
(QOS WIN 4–3 ON PENS)
Ibrox

Charles Green's days of receiving six of the best were long gone, but the Gers chief was again set to experience Scottish football's equivalent of being summoned to the headmaster's office after being served with a notice of complaint by the SFA. The charges related to comments he allegedly made regarding the integrity of a commission poised to investigate Rangers' use of Employee Benefit Trusts (EBTs). The three-man panel – chaired by Lord Nimmo Smith – was set up by the SPL to determine whether the club had breached rules relating to alleged undisclosed payments to players during Sir David Murray's tenure. Green refused to recognise or co-operate with the commission and was reported as saying, "That's what we're going to spend our time doing, not turning up at supposedly independent hearings where the SPL appoint the jury, set the outcome and set the punishment before we have the trial." Green was given until September 24 to respond. He didn't bother waiting. Instead, he immediately issued a statement citing his right to freedom of speech as his defence.

"We've made very clear that we have never questioned the integrity of the panel," he said. "That is beyond reproach. What I do have an issue with is the fact that the SPL has relentlessly been pursuing a fixed and predetermined agenda on EBTs from the moment they realised that they would not be able to get Rangers back into the SPL without a fan revolt. Until that moment, the

SPL were looking to trade SPL status for an admission of guilt on EBTs and a sanction of stripped titles. We couldn't and didn't give them that. What I'm doing is using free speech to tell the fans exactly what has happened and I am now on disrepute charges for matters of fact."

While dogged in their determination to retain past honours, Rangers were just as desperate to add to their haul of silverware. The last time they chased four trophies in one season was back in 2008 – four years earlier and a lifetime ago. League Cup, Scottish Cup, SPL title – and the UEFA Cup. The dream of a first European trophy since 1972 eventually died on May 15 that year at the hands of Dick Advocaat's Zenit St Petersburg in the City of Manchester Stadium after an epic run of nineteen ties. There was to be no championship success either, but the campaign did end on a high when Kris Boyd grabbed the winner in a closely fought contest with Queen of the South in the Scottish Cup final, as a weary Rangers side limped over the finish line in their sixty-eighth game of an arduous season. Fast forward to a different year, where a different quadruple was up for grabs, and the Dumfries side were again set to play a starring role.

It's claimed, with tongue firmly in cheek, that Queens are the only British football club to be mentioned in the Bible, where Luke 11:31 states, "The queen of the south will rise up at the judgement." Rangers headed into the Ramsdens Cup quarter-final hoping their own rise would continue.

Before the action got underway, silence fell over the

stadium as fans remembered the ninety-six who perished at Hillsborough. Like Liverpool, Rangers had also endured tragedy with the loss of sixty-six supporters in the 1971 Ibrox Disaster. On this cold, crisp evening in Glasgow, banners reflecting the loss suffered by both clubs fluttered in the centre circle before the teams emerged. It was a poignant reminder that football is only a game – but also of its ability to unite.

The Doonhamers had enjoyed an unbeaten start to the season under former Light Blues midfielder Allan 'Magic' Johnston, including an impressive victory over Hibernian in the League Cup. But despite their recent travel sickness, Rangers' results at Ibrox this season were convincing enough and recent history was also on their side. The last time Queens defeated the Govan club was back in 1955 in the old Scottish Division One, while historians had to go back further to 1948 to find their last triumph at Ibrox. Would history be written again or would Rangers continue their progression in an unfamiliar competition?

There was a blow for the hosts beforehand with the news that Templeton would be sidelined for a number of weeks with ankle ligament damage sustained at Annan. With top goalscorer Little also out of action with a foot problem, attacking options for McCoist were limited.

The Second Division leaders signalled their intent right from the outset. Alexander was made fully aware this was a night where he would have to earn his wages when he was called into action to block a smart shot from Chris Mitchell before tipping over the crossbar from Daniel Carmichael. Rangers offered nothing in the first half, with the majority of the 23,392 paying punters probably wishing they had stayed at home to watch the Champions League match between Real Madrid and Manchester City on the telly instead. The home players traipsed off to the sound of jeers at half-time and the boos were replaced by cheers from the away fans just four minutes into the second half.

The opener came courtesy of Nicky Clark, son of former Gers and Jambos striker Sandy, who was now part of the coaching staff at Palmerston. Willie Gibson was the provider with the cross from the left, as Clark connected to send a powerful downward header past Alexander. The goalkeeper then pulled a save from the top drawer to prevent a second goal for the man who shares his name with a celebrity hairdresser and who was finding it all too easy to cut the defence wide open. But it was the visiting rearguard who paid the price at the other end when failure to deal with Black's corner saw the ball break kindly for Barrie McKay to drive home from six yards ten minutes after the restart.

Kevin Kyle had replaced Sandaza but was given his marching orders after just thirteen minutes on the park for an apparent elbow on Ryan McGuffie. Despite the numerical disadvantage, Rangers edged in front when McCulloch was tripped in the box by Chris Higgins and the skipper dusted himself off to convert the spot-kick. The numbers were levelled when Gibson was also dismissed with two minutes of the regulation ninety to go. Arbroath, Cowdenbeath or Partick Thistle? Rangers were probably already wondering who they would face in the semi-final when they were hit with the sucker punch. Gavin Reilly's leveller deep into injury-time forced the tie into extra-time when the goal was allowed to stand despite furious appeals for offside.

A further thirty minutes failed to separate the sides and penalties beckoned. Shiels and Argyriou both failed to convert from twelve yards, before McGuffie netted the decisive strike. Queen of the South's unbeaten record for the season remained intact. Rangers' was obliterated. Speaking before the game, Sandaza had likened away games in the Third Division to a war and the hosts proved to be conscientious objectors in this particular battle on home territory.

For McCoist, the cup exit was down to nothing more than a bad day at the office. He said, "I don't think it's a wake-up call. It's certainly not a wake-up call for me – it's just a massive disappointment. We were all aware of how difficult the game would be against a good Queen of the South side, who are doing well in the league and who knocked Hibs out of the League Cup. If any of the boys needed a wake-up call, I hope that's it, but I don't think they were, to be honest. It's a sore one, that's for sure. It's really, really disappointing to get beat and get knocked out in the manner we did."

Johnston did not feel his old club underestimated the threat posed by his players, insisting, "Definitely not, they definitely prepared right for us. I know for a fact they had us watched and didn't underestimate us. I'm just delighted for our boys. With the effort they put in throughout the whole game, I think they got their just rewards come the end of the match."

SEPTEMBER 23, 2012
RANGERS 4   MONTROSE 1
Ibrox

The last couple of displays were enough to put years on anyone so it was no wonder McCoist revealed that he wanted a time machine when quizzed on the perfect gift for his impending fiftieth birthday. He didn't want to travel to the future to see how this Rangers journey back to the top would pan out. He didn't even want to go back to his days as a television personality when coming up with the answers to the picture round on *A Question of Sport* was as stressful as it got. If McCoist was ever going to pull off a Marty McFly stunt, there was only one place to go: back to his playing days. And with 355 strikes in all competitions for Rangers, the Ibrox faithful were probably wishing he could pull on his football boots again for the visit of Montrose.

According to some pundits and newspaper columns, the pressure was mounting on McCoist, the manager, as his side prepared to return to the scene of the crime. Deficiencies away from home this season, combined with an uninspiring record in knockout competitions since taking on the top job, meant the Light Blues boss should be feeling the heat, with fans beginning to lose patience with the current regime. That was the theory anyway. The reality was, in fact, a demonstration of support for McCoist in the shape of a giant tribute banner in the Broomloan Front, declaring, "We will follow in the footsteps of his team. Ally McCoist MBE. Player. Manager. Supporter. Legend." There was even a chorus of "Happy Birthday" just to hammer home the point.

McCoist didn't officially leave his forties behind until the following day and just how happy the milestone event would be was likely to depend on what Montrose had in their locker. Their boss, Stuart Garden, had form when it came to Rangers. The former Notts County shot-stopper enjoyed a hat-trick of wins over the club while employed as goalkeeping coach at Inverness, with two of those victories coming during Paul Le Guen's brief spell. Now he was seeking another scalp in his own right as boss of the Links Park outfit.

Sandaza was the only victim of the fall-out from the Queen of the South game, finding himself dumped on the subs' bench, while Faure was added to the side. Rangers had started previous games in a sluggish fashion and this tussle appeared to be no different. Montrose peppered the home goal with shots in the opening spell, with Argyriou supplying a heart-in-mouth moment when an attempted clearance rattled the woodwork. Rangers soothed frayed nerves when they opened the scoring after 27 minutes – the first time they had netted first in a league match at Ibrox this season. Shiels left his marker standing as he raced onto McCulloch's flick-on and drilled beyond goalkeeper David Crawford. The advantage was snuffed out just six minutes later. The Gable Endies restored parity when Ryan McIntosh punted a free-kick into the box and Argyriou, under pressure from Garry Wood, nodded past the helpless Alexander into his own net.

There was at least some light relief at the interval, with the launch of the Crossbar Challenge. £50,000 was up for grabs for any fan who could hit the crossbar from the centre circle, with the prize set to rise to a cool

£1 million for the final home game of the season against Berwick. On the basis of the first-half performance, McCoist might even have been tempted to throw in a two-year deal for today's hopeful if successful. Unfortunately, the chap in question barely managed to cover fifteen yards, with a Lotto scratch card on the way home providing a more realistic chance of finding his fortune than his football skills.

Just as well for Rangers that Lewis Macleod knew where the target was. The teenager opened his senior account for the club ten minutes into the second period when he ran onto a Faure pass, turned his marker and dispatched an angled drive into the bottom corner. Macleod then turned provider for lone frontman McCulloch to stab home on the hour mark. Another young starlet, Fraser Aird, replaced McKay to make his first-team debut and impressed by adding an injection of energy to the game. But it was another sub, Robbie Crawford, who provided the icing on the birthday cake when he claimed his first Rangers goal after just two minutes on the park.

"It's really important that the kids get an opportunity," stressed McCoist. "We have to get out of the division and we must win, but if we are going to get the chance to rebuild now would be an ideal time to blood the youngsters. We are asking these guys to come in and do men's jobs and at this moment in time they are doing it really well. These kids have been fabulous so far. We don't want to put too much pressure on them, but they are certainly exciting myself and they are great to work with."

However, the biggest challenge of the season so far was looming in the shape of high-flying Motherwell's visit in the League Cup – a match that would test young and old alike within the Rangers ranks. McCoist continued, "We are up against arguably the in-form team in the SPL at the moment. They are a handful. They gave us some really tough games when we had Nikica Jelavić and Allan McGregor and Steven Naismith and we were a team who were winning the SPL. They gave us tough games then so we are in for a tough game this time, but I would have to say that I think and hope the occasion would bring out the best in us."

For now, though, the manager could enjoy a result that allowed his side to move to within a point of the Division Three summit. It was far from being a champagne performance, but he could blow out his fifty candles safe in the knowledge the lights wouldn't be going out on his Rangers career just yet.

SEPTEMBER 26, 2012
RANGERS 2   MOTHERWELL 0
Ibrox

A sure-fire way for McCoist to silence his critics? How about dumping an SPL side out of the League Cup just a couple of months after Rangers were themselves dumped out of the SPL? The Motherwell board reached their own decision to reject the 'newco' Rangers bid for entry to the top flight after holding a ballot of 'Well Society members. The transition towards a fan ownership model meant club chiefs thought supporters should have the biggest say and a massive 82 per cent voted against allowing Rangers to remain in the SPL. However, Green was keen to extend the hand of friendship ahead of this game to a club he felt were under pressure from their own fans when submitting a "no" vote, stating he did not believe Motherwell were "anti-Rangers". He added ominously that other SPL clubs would not be made so welcome at Ibrox when the situation arose . . .

As for the Steelmen, they were keen to focus on a game of football rather than a summer of negotiations, a message which was conveyed in a statement of their own: "We are excited to be playing a Scottish Communities League Cup fixture against Rangers as both clubs build for the future. All of our focus should be on the field of play and we look forward to what promises to be a great game. We are pleased to note both the CEO and board of Rangers recently said they would welcome our staff and fans and we will extend the same courtesy to all clubs ourselves as we seek to create a welcoming family club. The past is done; we now can only influence the future. We are now totally focused on what happens on the field."

McCoist branded Motherwell favourites to come out on top, while 'Well boss Stuart McCall claimed his own side were underdogs heading into the tie. Mind games or not, this was a tough one to call. Rangers still boasted players who should be capable of competing at the top level, as well as a wage bill unrivalled by most other Scottish clubs, but were now a shadow of their former selves. Plus, the wounds from the Ramsdens Cup exit at the hands of Queen of the South were still raw. Motherwell's aversion to Rangers – and visits to Ibrox in particular – was starkly illustrated by their inability to overcome the blue half of the Old Firm in any of the previous thirty-eight encounters between the sides. James McFadden was the hero when he supplied the knockout blow in a Boxing Day battle the last time Motherwell triumphed in 2002, whereas the last victory in Govan was back in May 1997, when Owen Coyle stole the show with a double.

A remarkable opening to the current campaign saw McCall's men alight in the south side of Glasgow as SPL leaders, having clambered to the peak of the table thanks to an undefeated domestic run. European outings had proved more difficult to negotiate, after being catapulted into the role of Champions League representatives as a result of Rangers' insolvency. Home and away defeats to Greeks Panathinaikos in the qualifiers were followed by an early exit from the Europa League courtesy of Spanish side Levante – a record which was mocked by the Rangers fans in the form of an artistic piece of multi-lingual handiwork unfurled ahead of kick-off.

Sandaza was back in favour, while Aird made his first start after his promising bow, but the match ended abruptly and painfully for the Spaniard. A nauseating clash of heads with Shaun Hutchinson resulted in the Motherwell defender leaving the pitch with blood pouring from a wound, before eventually returning to the action after receiving stitches. But it was match over for a groggy-looking Sandaza, who was taken down the tunnel on a stretcher. Scans later revealed a fractured cheekbone and a facial injury so severe the striker almost lost an eye, with a three-month lay-off anticipated. Hospital-bound Sandaza was replaced on 24 minutes by Kyle Hutton, who had not been seen in a Light Blue jersey since the win over East Fife in early August.

The tie remained deadlocked at the break, when the biggest cheer of the night so far was reserved for Nacho Novo as he conducted the half-time draw. With the little Spanish striker back on the pitch and Motherwell in the away dressing room, it was almost like old times. The theme continued four minutes into the second half when Rangers asserted their authority over their Lanarkshire visitors. Aird's short corner was flighted into the box by Shiels and McCulloch took advantage of poor defending to power home a header from six yards. As the *Superman* theme tune blasted out from the PA system, the captain celebrated with a superhero-esque dive to the turf before being swamped by jubilant team-mates. All that was missing were the red pants and matching cape. Rangers doubled their lead when Argyriou squared to Shiels in plenty of space to volley past Darren Randolph.

"SPL, you're having a laugh," taunted the home support as Ibrox rocked. Under any other circumstances the sight of the SPL leaders being cast aside by a Division Three club would have been regarded as a momentous shock. On this occasion? Probably not. The venue held happy memories for McCall, the player, thanks to his seven trophy-laden years at Rangers – but was not a happy hunting ground as a manager.

"If you asked anybody who's watched Rangers all season, they've never played anything like that but it was always going to be the case," he said. "I was certainly aware of what we would face – it was their biggest game in terms of an SPL club coming here. But I look at my own side and we lost too many battles."

For Hutton, the victory was about more than mere progression in the cup or bragging rights over illustrious opponents. For the twenty-one-year-old midfielder, it was an opportunity to re-establish himself in the top team after claiming he had no idea why he had dropped out of McCoist's plans. "I've not really got an answer to that question," he said. "I could have sat in the corner and sulked but I knew what I had to do. I just kept my head down and worked hard. I got my reward and I took my chance so hopefully things can change. I've been a bit frustrated over the past while with not getting a game. I've come in now and played well so hopefully I can kick on now."

McCoist was more interested in what the result and performance said about the team as a whole. He said, "It's a wee indicator to ourselves and the support that we can play against teams from the top of the league and higher up in the divisions but we can't get carried away. It's a very small step on what's going to be a long road. I make no apologies for telling the supporters that – we've got miles and miles to go. But it shows you, in a one-off game, we can compete with anybody."

The grin was wiped off the manager's face when he returned home and settled down on the sofa with a cuppa and the Sky+ remote to watch the television coverage of the game. The only titles McCoist had ever been interested in were those of the championship variety, but he was furious with the opening title sequence of the BBC's *Sportscene* programme. He was already unhappy with a discussion about himself on the BBC Radio Scotland show *Off the Ball* the previous Saturday, entitled "Super Ally or Fat Sally". And he was apparently "disgusted" by an animated montage based on the opening credits of American television show *Mad Men*, at the beginning of *Sportscene*.

According to a club statement: "Rangers Football Club has lodged a formal complaint with the BBC following what it regards as a tasteless opening title sequence for last night's live League Cup TV coverage. The Light Blues have today been inundated with emails and phone calls from supporters who are – rightly, in our opinion – furious with the way the programme began. It started with an animated montage which depicted a Rangers official, clearly manager Ally McCoist, falling from an office window at Ibrox and smashing a club crest.

"The incident follows a discussion on BBC Radio Scotland show *Off the Ball* on Saturday entitled 'Super Ally or Fat Sally', which questioned whether fans still backed McCoist. While the manager is known for his good sense of humour, he is both angry and disgusted by the BBC's treatment both of him personally and of the club."

Green had stated beforehand that Motherwell were not anti-Rangers and BBC Scotland claimed they had no agenda against the club either. They responded, "We accept that the creative animation – however well intentioned – may not have appealed to everyone, but we would like to stress that there was no intention to cause any offence. We absolutely reject, however, any suggestions that we have an anti-Rangers bias."

SEPTEMBER 29, 2012
FORRES MECHANICS 0   RANGERS 1
Mosset Park

When McCoist said his side had miles and miles to go, he wasn't kidding. One hundred and seventy four of them, all the way to Moray. Rangers might be motoring after their Motherwell success, but Forres Mechanics were determined to put the brakes on their progress in the Scottish Cup. Another lengthy journey to the north of Scotland for the second-round tie meant another road trip and another bleary-eyed start for myself and Radio Clyde's Alison. Two girls in one car heading off on an adventure. It was just like *Thelma and Louise* – but hopefully without the driving off a cliff part.

Our own enthusiasm levels had yet to peak at such an early hour, but cup fever had been gripping the Royal Burgh for weeks. The possibility of switching the tie to Inverness' Caledonian Stadium twenty-five miles away was mooted before the decision was taken to host Rangers at the club's own little Mosset Park. Moray Council had even given the green light for the ground's capacity to be increased from 1,500 to 2,700 for the occasion by "making better use of the existing terrain" after a personal plea by Mechanics chairman Dr James Anderson. After season ticket holders, associated companies and Rangers Supporters Clubs had received their allocation of tickets, the remaining 400 briefs were snapped up in under ten minutes after going on general sale, with fans limited to two tickets each. Demand was clearly still outweighing the supply despite the additional 1,200 tickets, but hope was not completely lost for empty-handed (and hungry) locals.

Maclean's Highland Bakery launched a Willy Wonka-style giveaway, with hidden messages in specially wrapped Scotch pies, advising customers whether they had won a "Golden Ticket" for the visit of the Glasgow giants. There were six Charlie Bucket-style winners in total, with two tickets given away on each of the three days leading up to the big match. According to head baker Lewis Maclean, "Pie sales had been going bananas."

Supporters weren't the only ones determined not to miss out on the tie. Forres captain Ross MacPherson had been booked to go on holiday the same weekend as the game and scrapped the trip to Magaluf in order to face the Gers instead. The decision meant writing off £500, but according to the midfielder, playing in the game would be "well worth it – the chance of a lifetime". Having recently led the club to the Highland League championship for only the second time in their 128-year history, the Celtic fan was now hoping for a famous double by adding a major cup scalp to the list of achievements. The optimism was shared by Forres' official website, which declared, "They said it was unique. They said it could be tough for Rangers. They said Forres are Highland League Champions. They said Rangers have had Forres watched! They said it was a dream tie. They said we had a chance. WE SAID – BRING IT ON!" McCoist confirmed Rangers had, indeed, had Forres watched. Three times. The manager was desperate to prevent Mechanics throwing a spanner in the works, warning his players, "Don't become a statistic."

Speaking of statistics . . .

Forres Mechanics were established in 1884, twelve years after Rangers, and were one of the seven founder members of the Highland Football League. They have played at Mosset Park since 1886 and, until now, had not hosted either side of the Old Firm at the venue since 1957. The only previous meeting with Rangers was in a friendly in 1908. Most of the players hold down full-time jobs – manager Charlie Rowley is a plumber by trade – but you don't have to spend your working day under a car bonnet to play for the Mechanics. The origins of such a unique name were explained in Colin G. Watson's book *Forres Mechanics: The First Hundred Years*, when describing the October 1884 meeting convened to set up a new club.

The book stated, "The only common factor between those present was that they were all 'Mechanics'. This did not mean that they all tinkered with the latest Ford or Rover model off the assembly line as these were still far in the future. They were simply, as defined in the Oxford English Dictionary, 'people who are employed in manual occupation; and craftsmen'."

The town itself has a population of 9,000 and is situated on the shores of the Moray Firth. In fictional terms, it is the location for Duncan's castle in the Shakespeare play *Macbeth*. In reality, Forres is a picturesque town probably best known for its floral sculptures and displays, which have resulted in a number of Scotland in Bloom awards and even earned the prestigious Britain in Bloom Medium Town Trophy in 2004. Other attractions include Sueno's Stone, white sandy beaches, dolphin sightings, the Dallas Dhu and Benromach Distilleries and fishing in the Findhorn River. On this particular day, though, there was only one show in town.

With a number of private properties overlooking the three open sides to the ground, ticketless fans watched from house windows, congregated in gardens and clambered onto fences to witness the action. One chap on a giant trampoline in one of the gardens even gave new meaning to the phrase "doing the bouncy". As for Gers chief Green, he had one of the best seats in the house in the front row of the main stand, bang in the centre. The Press didn't do too badly either. This should have been the kind of match that brings hacks out in a cold sweat as they fret over filing copy and meeting deadlines under tough working conditions, as laptop batteries die and dongles fail to pick up a signal. Instead, there was fully functioning Wi-Fi and brand new power points installed in the back row of the stand, which had been allocated to journalists for the day. The social club doubled up as a press room, with friendly staff providing delicious homemade soup and sandwiches before kick-off and home baking – including blue frosted cupcakes – post-match. It was mentioned more than once by the assembled media that a few SPL clubs could learn a thing or two from Forres in terms of the warm welcome afforded to their visitors and the military planning which had gone into making sure the day went as smoothly as possible.

Clearly the meticulous planning had extended to on-field preparations too. The Can Cans had a decent penalty claim dismissed with less than a minute on the clock when a Scott Moore drive appeared to hit the arm of Faure. Rangers made two changes from the win over Motherwell, with Kal Naismith earning his first start, and Hutton also added to the side in place of crocked duo Sandaza and Shiels. Naismith marked the occasion with his first Rangers goal when he rifled home following a cross from the left from the lively Aird. If the visitors thought the floodgates would open after the fourteenth-minute opener, they were sadly mistaken. Even Nathan Sharp's red card for deliberate handball on 66 minutes failed to aid Rangers' cause and they only just managed to scrape through to the third round with an uncon-vincing 1–0 victory. Forres were the better team in the second half and few who witnessed the match – regardless of allegiance – would have begrudged them a money-spinning replay at Ibrox.

Alexander admitted he had expected a goal-fest against the non-league outfit – only to find himself worked harder than Forres number 1 Stuart Knight. "If I'm being brutally honest, it was a poor performance away from home again from us," said the Rangers keeper. "We knew it was going to be hard, it's a tough place to come to. They came out with all guns blazing and made it really hard for us to play. All credit to them; maybe in all honesty they deserved something out of the game. We thought we would create all the pressure and maybe score three, four, five goals. But we just didn't get to grips with the game and that's all credit to them – I thought they were fantastic. We kept giving away free-kicks and letting them put pressure on us. We found it hard to get any real rhythm to our game and we didn't really create any opportunities and work their goalie. I think I was probably the harder-worked goalie, which shouldn't be. We should be coming to these teams and scoring a lot of goals and putting on a show. It didn't happen for whatever reason."

Alexander revealed that McCoist had given his players "a right rollicking" afterwards and the Gers boss blasted, "It was a relief to get through because we weren't good. It's obviously a bit of a helter-skelter we're on at the moment this season and that was evident. I don't think I would be doing my job if I didn't register my disappointment at the way we played and passed the ball."

Rowley was also disappointed for very different reasons. "It was a very disappointed dressing room and I think that says it all about how well we played," he said. "I asked them to give their all and I'm proud of my players."

To their credit, everyone involved with Forres Mechanics gave their all to ensure a memorable occasion would be remembered for all the right reasons. They were winners off the park, even if the result wasn't the one they wanted – or deserved – in the end. It was the tie the whole town craved and they relished every minute of it. Confession time: my own heart sank when the draw was made and I realised I would have to add another remote Scottish outpost to my list of far-flung destinations on the road with Rangers this season. But, do you know what? It was the best experience so far – by 174 miles. So forget the flowers and the whisky. If you ever find yourself in Forres, make sure that Mosset Park tops the list of places to visit. TripAdvisor take note.

OCTOBER

Something Borrowed, Something Blue

OCTOBER 6, 2012
STIRLING ALBION 1   RANGERS 0
Forthbank

The first ever competitive meeting between Forres and Rangers was marked with an exchange of gifts between the two clubs. Forres presented their visitors with a specially commissioned plate depicting twenty-two sheep in the colours of both teams playing a game of football, with the town's iconic Nelson Tower in the background. In return for the unique offering, Rangers opted for a more traditional "gift of friendship" in the shape of an elegant engraved cut-glass decanter. Rangers travelled to Stirling Albion knowing they couldn't be quite so generous in bearing gifts to their hosts on this occasion, at least as far as points were concerned.

The Scottish Cup win, albeit away from home and on unfamiliar terrain, had done little to ease the pressure to deliver a first league victory on the road. There was a demand to get the monkey off the back before the monkey became a gorilla, and any betting man would have put his mortgage on the visit to Forthbank as being the match where McCoist's men turned the corner. In saying that, having now had my fingers burned twice as a result of my gambling habits this season (the coupon for a rather optimistic 80/1 shot on Rangers winning the quadruple had also ended up in the bin) I was making sure I still had a roof over my head come the end of the day.

Albion headed into the encounter rooted to the bottom of the table and on a poor run of five straight defeats in Division Three, while victory for the visitors from Glasgow would propel them to the summit. As well as current form, past results also favoured Rangers in this fixture. The Binos' only previous victory was back in September 1953 at their old Annfield home in a Division One match. Willie Woodburn scored an own-goal and was later sent off before Dick Whitehead netted to secure a 2–0 win over Bill Struth's Rangers. More recent encounters had proved enjoyable for current boss McCoist, who was one of the scorers in a 3–2 League Cup victory at Ibrox in the last competitive meeting between the sides in 1995. He was also on target in another League Cup win at Brockville in 1987. This time around, McCoist would be in the dugout, but the same could not be said for Stirling player-boss Greig McDonald. He was set to miss one of the biggest games since the club's inception in 1945 for a big day of his own – his wedding. His nuptials to fiancée Jennifer were already booked well before he replaced Jocky Scott at the helm and became Scottish football's youngest manager at the age of twenty-nine in January 2012.

"It was already booked and agreed with the board and everything was fine," said McDonald. "It was ages in advance and the game was against Stranraer. Then it turned out it was actually going to be against Rangers, such is life, and it was the ultimate test for me. What comes first – my wife or my football? Clearly, my wedding day was more important and I had the ultimate faith in my assistants, Marc McCulloch and Shaun Fagan, and the players to carry on as normal.

"I would never have switched the wedding day – I would have been killed for that! There was talk at the time that the game may go live to TV and be a noon kick-off, which would have worked well. I was getting married about half an hour away from the stadium and I could have taken the game and then went straight to the wedding for the ceremony. But they decided not to televise it and stuck with the 3pm kick-off."

Throw in the fact the match was taking place at Albion's compact, modern stadium – their home since 1993 – on a reasonable playing surface, which should suit the visitors, and Rangers were almost certain to end their away day woes. Weren't they?

If further incentive was needed, it had arrived in the shape of Stirling secretary Dick King's resignation the month before. The club official stood down from his position after sparking outrage among fans of both clubs by making derogatory comments about Rangers supporters on an unofficial fans' forum, where he reportedly referred to them as "the Huns". His resignation was followed by a statement, which read, "I apologise unreservedly for remarks which I made on a Stirling

Albion unofficial website in respect of Rangers FC. In so doing, I am removing myself forthwith from any further involvement with Stirling Albion FC in any capacity. I hope that both clubs will now be able to move forward unbesmirched by my actions and I wish them well for the future."

Operations director Stuart Brown added, "I would wish to assure Rangers FC and their fans that nothing apart from the hand of friendship will be extended to them at Forthbank Stadium on 6 October, and indeed at any time. We have a very close and healthy relationship with Rangers that has been built up over many years and I fervently hope that this isolated and unacceptable incident will not serve to impact detrimentally on this. We have the utmost respect for the Club and their supporters and I have been particularly impressed by the manner in which Charles Green, his associates, and, perhaps most significantly, their fans have handled themselves during what has been an extremely difficult period in their proud Club's history."

Referee Bobby Madden led the teams and his officials out onto the pitch past a pipe and drum guard of honour. There was no sign of Colin Hendry or Mel Gibson in the 3,800 crowd, but there was definitely more than a hint of *Braveheart* about the occasion. Albion were shooting into the end which was overlooked by the Wallace Monument, the famous structure commemorating the thirteenth-century Scottish hero William Wallace.

Eight minutes into the match, the town had a new hero and his name was Brian Allison. Daly McSorley's inswinging corner sparked confusion in the box and

Allison took advantage of poor defending to fire high into the net from close range. He must have felt as high as a kite and as dizzy as the visitors who regularly climb the 246 steps of a spiral staircase to reach the top of the Monument. As well as the unseeing eyes of Wallace, the action also took place under the watchful gaze of Charles Green – whose charges of bringing the game into disrepute over comments relating to the SPL's EBT commission were found to be "not proven" by the SFA. He sat with Head of Football Administration Andrew Dickson, Sandy Jardine and Andy Cameron in the packed main stand. But even the veteran comedian would struggle to see the funny side of what was unfolding on the park in front of him.

Finding themselves trailing was not exactly a new experience for Rangers this season, and Lee McCulloch's header scraped the inside of the post as they tried to force their way back into the match. But the Glasgow giants could not find the goal to prevent a shock first defeat in Division Three as the home support – out-numbered by travelling fans – celebrated a famous victory at the final whistle. The win was all the more spectacular for Stirling when it emerged post-match that goalkeeper Sam Filler played part of the first half with vision in just one eye following a clash with McCulloch. With blood seeping from his mouth at the break, he was replaced by Mark Peat, who did a convincing enough impression of the number 1 in the second half that many observers were initially unaware that a change had even taken place at half-time.

With McDonald getting hitched, it was left to his

assistants to ensure the game went without a hitch. Marc McCulloch helped pull the strings on the pitch, while Shaun Fagan dished out the orders on the touchline. Speaking beforehand, McCulloch insisted, "Come 3pm, we must believe anything can happen." Fagan revealed afterwards that one young player, Stephen Day, was still sitting in the dressing room refusing to change out of his strip as the result slowly began to sink in.

As for the other McCulloch, all Rangers captain Lee could offer was an apology to fans, who again headed home weighted down by a sense of disappointment tinged with embarrassment. He said, "We owed a result to the fans, who turned up and made it another sell-out. We can only apologise to them. We've got a lot of new players, a lot of young players, a couple of foreign players, who don't speak English. But that's all excuses, isn't it? It's not acceptable so we are going to have to respond to it."

McCoist – who was given Green's "100 per cent backing" despite the "unacceptable" defeat – made a point of waiting until the following day before picking over the game again. For a grand total of eight quid Stirling fans would soon be able to watch the match action as many times as they wanted. The club shop was stocked with commemorative mugs and pennants before the match and, with a "momentous" (their word) victory now in the bag, Albion were set to release a DVD of the full ninety minutes in time for Christmas, telling fans, "What better way to spend the festive period than by reliving one of the most remarkable matches in our history?"

For player-boss McDonald, the win proved to be the ideal wedding gift, with Rangers providing "something blue" on the big day. He said, "Most people were checking phones when we were getting the wedding photographs taken. When my best man told me we had scored, I thought he was winding me up because it was so early in the game. I honestly thought he was kidding. From then on, because we had scored, everybody was checking their phones. Every time I walked past somebody, they were telling me it was still 1–0. My focus that day was to make sure Jen enjoyed her day and that we both enjoyed the day. It turned out to be a perfect present for us."

OCTOBER 20, 2012
RANGERS 2   QUEEN'S PARK 0
Ibrox

Suffering defeat to a side rock bottom of the table and succumbing to one of the more lamentable results of the last 140 years was just one of the downsides to life in Scottish football's bottom tier. Another was the temporary absence of the Old Firm derby. A cup draw pairing the two rivals together was a possibility but Rangers and Celtic would not lock horns in league competition for at least a further two campaigns – barring any drastic reconstruction plans that catapulted the blue half of Glasgow back into the top flight earlier than anticipated. It was a fixture that Hoops majority shareholder Dermot Desmond admitted he would miss, while hailing Rangers as one of Britain's great clubs and highlighting their importance to Scottish football as a result of "their following, the size of the club and especially their history". The comments were welcomed by McCoist, who confessed he would also miss the rivalry with their fiercest foes over the coming seasons. He said, "I'm missing the Old Firm game. I think people who know what the Old Firm game is about and appreciate it will miss it. I don't think there is any doubt about that. One or two people say they don't miss it but I'm not sure they understand the Old Firm game and what it's about. If Dermot Desmond misses it, I've got to tell you that I miss it."

Rangers would not, however, be starved of city rivalry while in Division Three. Twelve years before the inaugural Old Firm match even took place, Rangers faced Queen's Park for the first time in the original Glasgow derby. The fixture first appeared in the record books in 1875 when the south-side clubs participated in a charity match, with proceeds going to the Bridgeton Fire Fund for families affected by a huge blaze in the city.

"The first meeting between the two sides was a long, long time ago, way before my time," said Rangers historian Robert McElroy. "It was in November 1875; Queen's Park won 2–0 at the first Hampden Park, which is now a bowling green. Back then, although Rangers had been in existence for three years prior to that game, Queen's wouldn't play them until Rangers had their own ground. They had a policy of not playing clubs who didn't have their own grounds at that time. By 1875 Rangers did have their own ground at Burnbank so Queen's gave them a game.

"Moving forward to April 1877 and the first

competitive game between the clubs was in the Charity Cup. The big one in Rangers' early years was the Scottish Cup in 1879. It was their first Scottish Cup tie and it was also Rangers' first win over Queen's Park, and that was quite an achievement. The Rangers player Willie Dunlop scored the only goal and later revealed he had actually bet a sovereign on Queen's Park to win the Scottish Cup, so he cost himself money."

The intervening decades had, of course, seen Rangers and Celtic both surpass Queen's and establish themselves as the superpowers of Scottish football, but the role played by the amateur outfit, not only in Scotland, but in the game as a whole, is certainly worthy of mention. The country's oldest organised football club was born at a meeting held on July 9, 1867, with the minutes of the gathering stating, "Tonight at half past eight o'clock a number of gentlemen met at No.3 Eglinton Terrace for the purpose of forming a football club."

The rest, as they say, is history.

Queen's had a pivotal role to play in establishing the SFA. They organised and supplied the entire team for the first international between Scotland and England under Association rules, and they also featured twice in the FA Cup before the introduction of the Scottish Cup. Even more impressively, the Spiders introduced new concepts to football, such as crossbars, half-time and free-kicks, which were all later incorporated into the modern game. The club also decided that their players would not be paid and adopted the motto: *Ludere Causa Ludente* – to play for the sake of playing. To this day, players have never received a wage from the Spiders.

Now, 137 years after the first meeting between Rangers and Queen's Park, the oldest derby in the world was set to be resurrected. "This season is the first time that I can recall seeing Rangers play Queen's Park in a league game," said McElroy. "When I was a wee boy, I may have been at one but I can't remember. The last league game was in February 1958 and Rangers beat Queen's Park 5–1. Since then, I've seen them in League Cup and Scottish Cup ties. This game has been very cleverly billed as the original Glasgow derby, which it was."

After the setback in Stirling, McCoist didn't just roll up his sleeves for this encounter; he ditched the club suit altogether in favour of his training gear. The smart attire was gone but the message was loud and clear that the manager meant business. The appearance of a track-suited McCoist in the dugout sparked furious debate on the Internet among suddenly fashion conscious fans, with some clearly not happy that the traditional collar and tie combo had been discarded.

The manager explained, "The match-day suit is taken off prior to kick-off and put back on immediately after the final whistle. The thinking behind it was that I wanted the players to look over to the side and see me in my working gear, same as they are. I understand totally the collar and tie thing with the older Rangers supporters. There have been one or two comments from the fans — but there's nobody more respectful than me of the club's history. I'm not saying I won't go back to the suit. It is getting colder."

Rangers made one change with Kyle Hutton replacing

Anestis Argyriou in the starting XI. Andy Little was back in contention after a six-week absence with a foot injury and was named among the substitutes. "In the past, I've had little injuries and big injuries as well," said the striker. "I was always frustrated, as anyone would be. But I've never felt frustration like I have this season. In the past I wasn't playing and I was trying to get myself back on the bench or maybe get a sub appearance. This season when I've been fit I've pretty much played and that's been brilliant for me and what I needed. It's been frustrating and the main reason it's been frustrating is because if I was fit I would have been playing those games."

The home side began the day in fourth spot, while Queen's made the short trip across the city for the clash at Ibrox in pole position in SFL3. The amateurs attempted to turn the clock back to a time when they were the dominant force between the two sides and gave as good as they got in a first half that ended goalless despite chances for both sides. Hutton and Ian Black were involved in a brief argument as the teams walked off at the break, with McCulloch later revealing those were not the only raised voices in the dressing room at half-time.

It was the captain who provided the opener after 57 minutes, when Dean Shiels squared for McCulloch to tap home into the unguarded net. Andrew Robertson then spurned a wonderful opportunity to restore parity. A one-two with Jamie Longworth put the winger clean through on goal with the ball on his left foot, but he delayed his shot, which allowed Neil Alexander to narrow the angle sufficiently to block his shot from eight yards. Another simple finish for McCulloch in injury-time after Barrie McKay's thirty-yard drive bounced back off the bar provided Rangers with a score-line that suggested a more comfortable victory than it actually was. Queen's Park's last win at Ibrox was back in 1948 and for all their endeavour they were unable to repeat that feat on this occasion.

The victory, albeit unconvincing, allowed Rangers to move top of the pile for the first time this season. McCoist said, "I hope there is a realisation coming from everyone about the players we have lost and they realise it's not going to be an overnight fix. But that's us top of the league now and I'm hoping we can now push through the mental barrier and kick on now."

The 49,463 attendance was again hailed as a world record for a fourth-tier match, this time by the stadium announcer. The crowd was second only to Manchester United's full house against Stoke in the UK, while Celtic played out their 5–0 win over St Mirren in nearby Paisley in front of 6,008 folk.

McCoist added, "It's an unbelievable attendance and there's something not right about it. Time will tell if the attendances will stay high but the first sign of their backing was when we got 36,000 season tickets sold in the space of five days. That in itself was phenomenal. People have used the word 'defiance' before about the fans but I think the word we should use is 'support', because that's what they are giving us."

McCulloch felt a frank exchange of views at the interval helped Rangers grind out the win, saying, "There were four or five different arguments, and we were all getting uptight. It just shows there are a lot of winners in the dressing room, that 0–0 at half-time is annoying the players and they expect more from each other. I think that showed in the second half with the way we played. I think it's a healthy thing if boys are arguing, as long as it's not getting ridiculous, which it isn't. It just shows a will to win."

Such a will to win would be tested again the following week with a visit to Clyde providing another opportunity to nail down that elusive first away win in the league. McCulloch added, "Everyone knows our away form has been nowhere near good enough. If we treat next week like a cup final and get a positive result, then we can certainly try to kick on from there as well."

OCTOBER 28, 2012
CLYDE 0   RANGERS 2
Broadwood

Once upon a time, Clyde were regulars in real cup finals, winning the Scottish Cup three times, finishing as runners-up on a further three occasions and boasting numerous appearances in the final of the Glasgow Cup.

During that period they were another team who could be considered city rivals of Rangers, having begun life at Barrowfield Park on the banks of the River Clyde in 1877 before a long residency at Shawfield Stadium in nearby Rutherglen. It all went a bit downhill for the Bully Wee when they were served notice by the ground's owners, The Greyhound Racing Association, and eventually played their last game at the venue in 1986, as

Shawfield became more commonly associated with "the dugs". The homeless years followed, and spells ground-sharing with Partick Thistle and Hamilton resulted in their supporters becoming known as "The Gypsy Army", before Clyde eventually settled in Cumbernauld in 1994. So, what is there to say about the North Lanarkshire "new town", which has been the home of the Bully Wee for the last nineteen years?

The Good: Cumbernauld was the location for *Gregory's Girl*, the charming 1981 Scottish coming-of-age romantic comedy, which remains one of just a handful of films with a football theme that actually makes for decent viewing. Unfortunately McCoist's own debut movie, *A Shot at Glory*, was a little less successful at the box office. The Bad: Cumbernauld shot to prominence for all the wrong reasons in 2005 when it featured on the Channel 4 series *Demolition* and the entire town centre earned a public nomination for demolition. This, of course, did not happen, although the centre has since been titivated up a bit. The Ugly: Cumbernauld won an architecture magazine's Plook on the Plinth Award for being Scotland's "most dismal town" in both 2001 and 2005 – the latter of which was also the year Clyde and Rangers last faced each other. Doubles from Thomas Buffel and Federico Nieto, and a Marvin Andrews goal secured a 5–2 win in extra-time in a League Cup tie. The stakes were just as high this time around.

Little made his first start since the beginning of September, after an encouraging substitute appearance against Queen's Park, while Chris Hegarty was also added to the side. Fraser Aird dropped to the bench and Sébastien Faure was absent from the team sheet. It proved to be a good weekend for the Shiels family when Dean opened the scoring in style twenty-four hours after his dad, Kenny, guided Kilmarnock to an historic victory at Celtic Park. The deadlock was broken after seventeen minutes when the attacking midfielder unleashed an unstoppable right-foot shot into the top corner. Stefan McCluskey should have levelled for Clyde but somehow managed to drag just wide of target with the gaping net at his mercy. It was the sort of miss the striker will no doubt watch over and over again, like a recent divorcee might watch the video of his wedding day and ponder where it went wrong. However, John Neill had a bigger part to play in the final outcome when he was needlessly dismissed after 68 minutes for clashing with Shiels. It was a moment of madness that tipped the match even further in Rangers' favour and McCulloch made sure the three points would be heading back to Ibrox with ten minutes to go when the unmarked utility man forced home Black's deep cross.

McCoist claimed their first away win was proof that Rangers were no longer willing to be the soft touches of the Third Division. He said, "If I'm playing against Rangers in SFL3, one of the first questions I would ask is, 'Do they fancy it? Let's have a look and see if they're up for the battle.' The vast majority of the football public might think we do have better players than SFL3 but, that said, you've got to earn the right to play. If somebody doesn't want to let you play and is aggressive, you have to combat that. You have to face up to it and match it. I do not have a problem at all with the level of competition and aggression that's been shown towards our team. The wee problem we probably had is we've not matched up to it – and we're maybe doing that now."

Bully Wee boss Jim Duffy knew the elusive away victory would come sooner or later and felt the facilities on offer at Broadwood helped Rangers' cause. He said, "You're thinking that they've not kicked into gear yet and you're just hoping there is another game to go before they do kick into gear. It's not going to last forever and I knew, for all the thoughts about playing on artificial surfaces, that Broadwood has as good a 3G surface as you will get.

"It's a really good environment to play in. I knew when Rangers came here they would enjoy passing the ball and playing on the surface. If you've got a dry, bumpy pitch or a muddy pitch and there are tight dressing rooms and the stadium is not the best, then it might just put a seed of doubt in their minds that they're not looking forward to it. But I think Rangers looked forward to playing at Broadwood and, although we played well, they just had that bit of extra quality.

"I think what Rangers needed was to win away from home. You've broken down the barrier and you can move forward. People stop talking about your record and the players start to believe they can win anywhere. At any level of football once you break down that barrier, once you get that belief back in camp, and you've got the best players in the league as well, there's only one way you're going to go and you're going to stride forward. There are defining games in the season in every league and, for Rangers, this was probably their defining game."

He added, "I think they had to adapt mentally and that's understandable. I thought they would win the league convincingly – and they will win it convincingly – but I didn't think they would fly out of the traps. If you watch football down south, for instance, if a team is relegated from the Premier League, it's rare that they will hit the ground running. So, it was understandable in the first couple of months that it took Rangers a bit of time to adjust. I don't think they had to adjust to the football side, I think it was more mentally, to basically resign themselves to where they are and deal with it."

Rangers had remedied their travel sickness but there was something else in the air down Govan way, and apparently it was highly infectious. It was a condition called "Rangers-itis" and the only known cure was the stirring notes of the famous Champions League anthem. Green had never made any secret of his desire to get the club back onto a secure financial footing, make a few quid along the way, and then move on. But, according to the businessman, Rangers had got under his skin and he indicated he might just stick around a bit longer than he initially anticipated.

"I am Rangers," he told listeners of *talkSPORT*. "I'm running that club, I'm making the decisions and I'm going to protect that club with my life. No one's ever going to abuse it. I've started to catch Rangers-itis. What I do see now is an opportunity to finish it and take it back to greatness. I won't leave before Champions League music's playing at Ibrox."

OCTOBER 31, 2012
RANGERS 0   INVERNESS CALEDONIAN THISTLE 3
Ibrox

Unfortunately for Rangers, the only strains of Tony Britten's 1992 composition to be heard in Glasgow this season would be coming from the east end of the city. While Celtic would be dining at Europe's top table with the likes of Benfica, Spartak Moscow and Barcelona, Rangers were hungry for further success in the League Cup. The victory over Motherwell in the last round was arguably the best of the season so far but, with another SPL outfit in the shape of Inverness providing the opposition this time, would we witness another Dr Jekyll display – or would Mr Hyde make an appearance on this dark and dank Halloween night?

Unsurprisingly, McCoist selected the same eleven players who defeated Clyde and it was the home side who began smartly at Ibrox, with Shiels, Little and Lewis Macleod all threatening in the opening exchange. Rangers certainly had enough incentives to come out on top. Earlier in the day skipper McCulloch penned a new two-year deal, while the 'oldco' Rangers formally entered liquidation. Insolvency firm BDO were appointed to wind up the company, now known as RFC 2012 plc, bringing to an end the period of administration.

Now was the perfect time for Rangers to inch forward another step and show that their focus was firmly trained on the future – except they didn't bargain for being haunted by ghosts of the past. Andrew Shinnie – once on the books at Rangers – fired the Highlanders ahead on

27 minutes when he ran onto an Aaron Doran pass before picking his spot and planting the ball beyond Alexander. Inverness were already on an unbeaten run of seven games and the opener simply fuelled their belief further. If the first half had been reasonably evenly matched, the second half amounted to little more than damage limitation for the hosts. The other Shinnie brother, Graeme, floated a corner into the box and the Gers' defence failed to react as Gary Warren directed a free header into the net on the hour mark. Graeme joined Andrew on the score sheet when he sent Alexander the wrong way from the penalty spot with just over ten minutes to go after his sibling was fouled by Argyriou. The win allowed Caley Thistle to advance to the semi-finals of the competition for the first time. Never mind "Rangers-itis", the Light Blues had just been given a large dose of something else – reality.

"I'm extremely aware of how far we've got to travel," said McCoist. "There is a thin line because it's difficult in the respect that I will never make excuses. I will not make excuses for the second-half performance and I won't make excuses for the slackness in defending at the three goals. But we have got a long way to go and this game showed that."

His views were echoed by McCulloch, whose earlier delight at his new deal had clearly been tempered by the cup exit. He said, "Maybe it was a bit of a reality check about how far we've got to go to get back to where we were. It's going to be a long road and it's going to take a bit of hard work to get there. It shows we won't be getting carried away with ourselves. We are just bitterly disappointed to be out of the cup. With a crowd of 28,000 coming here, with it being Halloween, a cold night, raining – they deserved better than what we showed. We just didn't seem to get going."

Terry Butcher milked the victory for all it was worth, with lavish celebrations on the final whistle. The former captain was used to enjoying the acclaim of the Ibrox faithful during his four years at Rangers but tonight made a beeline for the 300 or so fans who made the long journey south from the Highlands.

Butcher denied he was rubbing salt in the raw wounds of the home support, insisting, "I would hope no one would take offence. We have supporters who have to travel a very long way to see away matches and I was only inviting them to savour this moment. The celebrations were a reward for their loyalty to the club. I know how Ally will be feeling and I'm sorry for him."

NOVEMBER

Elgin Lose Their Marbles

NOVEMBER 3, 2012
RANGERS 7   ALLOA ATHLETIC 0
Ibrox

Harold Wilson once claimed that a week is a long time in politics, but it would appear that a year in football can completely change the landscape of the game. Remember, remember the 5th of November 2011? A brace from Nikica Jelavić inspired a 3–1 win over Dundee United to launch Rangers 15 points clear of Celtic in the SPL.

It was the high point of Ally McCoist's fledgling managerial career to date and those who savoured the victory at Ibrox could not even have begun to imagine what was to come in the weeks and months ahead for the defending champions. It was the halcyon days before the points advantage was eroded by the Hoops, before top marksman Jelavić was sold to Everton in a bargain £6 million sale that smacked of desperation by the Rangers owner, before the full extent of Craig Whyte's

financial shenanigans were laid bare and before the collapse of a football giant generated headlines around the
globe. Fast forward twelve months and, with two days
to go until Bonfire Night, Rangers fans still demanded
fireworks from a team who had since dragged themselves
from the smouldering embers of a disastrous regime.

Alloa were the visitors in the third round of the
Scottish Cup, as Rangers sought to continue their interest
in at least one cup competition this season, while avoid-
ing a second ignominious exit from a tournament in the
space of a few days. In short, McCoist's men needed to
respond positively to the midweek horror show against
Inverness. Jekyll or Hyde – who would turn up for this
one?

Lee Wallace was unavailable for selection with a dead
leg, while Kyle Hutton dropped to the bench, clearing the
way for Anestis Argyriou and Fraser Aird to start in front
of a crowd of 25,478. Lee McCulloch and Dean Shiels
provided the attacking threat as the manager deployed a
solid 4-4-2 formation. A 1–0 victory and a place in the
draw for the next round would probably have sufficed
against a Wasps side who no doubt fancied their own
chances, having witnessed the achievements of fellow
Second Division high-fliers Queen of the South and
Inverness in knockout competitions at the same venue.

But Paul Hartley's side were never given the chance to
get to grips with the tie and found themselves behind
with less than two minutes on the clock. Aird's corner
broke for Shiels, whose deflected shot found its way
through a sea of bodies before nestling in the bottom
corner. The blistering start was a sign of what was to

come. The Northern Irishman claimed a second when he collected a low pass from McCulloch and the offside flag stayed down as Shiels slid past Scott Bain. The captain then helped himself to a goal of his own with a powerful strike from just inside the box.

There was a setback when Argyriou was carried off after slumping to the turf holding his ankle. He was replaced by Robbie Crawford, as Andy Little switched to right-back before Barrie McKay added further pace to the proceedings when he took over from fellow youngster Aird. The changes provided little more than brief respite for Alloa, who fell further behind when McCulloch completed his double with a simple tap-in, before deputising for the injured Emílson Cribari in defence. The kids took over the goal-scoring duties from the experienced campaigners when Crawford supplied a low finish from Shiels' cut-back to add to the goal haul. McKay then applied a lavish coating of gloss to the win with a late brace as Alloa – whose numbers were reduced with ten minutes to go by Michael Doyle's red card for an impromptu boxing match with Chris Hegarty – were left dazed by the experience. By the end of the ninety minutes Rangers had five players aged twenty or under on the park but had gone one better than the last Scottish Cup tie between the clubs back in February 1994, which ended with a 6–0 rout.

For McCoist, it was a flashback to the days when ruthless Rangers sides had no qualms about destroying the opposition. Fans of other clubs had cruelly labelled the Light Blues "zombies" following their emergence from financial insolvency, but the manager saw more comparisons with the undead rather than the living dead, as he urged his players to go for the jugular. He said, "You just ask the players to take responsibility and believe in themselves a little bit and try to have a killer instinct – to want to score goals and be ruthless. I felt once we got the fourth goal we showed a streak that we haven't seen before and that was a desire to really go and score more goals. You were certainly entitled to expect good Rangers sides in the past to be ruthless. When they smelled blood they went for it. I would cut our boys a little bit of slack because a lot of them are new to the club and new to first-team football. But very good Rangers teams were very clinical."

Shiels didn't just want to smell blood, he wanted to smell fear from the opposition when they pitched up at Ibrox, admitting, "Our home form has been good but there have been times when we haven't been ruthless enough in front of goal and maybe defending our own goal. I think when you go three or four goals up, you've just got to keep going and try to get the next goal. It will make teams not want to come here and play here – that's the aim."

NOVEMBER 10, 2012
RANGERS 2   PETERHEAD 0
Ibrox

For all Shiels' fighting talk, Peterhead probably couldn't wait to have another crack at Rangers. The Blue Toon impressed on the opening day and would have made the long trip south in the hope that their efforts at Balmoor were simply the trailer for the main event on the big stage at Ibrox. Rangers were also keen to put on a show, with Charles Green hoping to persuade potential investors to plough their cash into the club as part of a share issue aimed at raising around £20 million. The Gers chief was set to embark upon an "investor road-show" the following week before the launch on the AIM market on the London Stock Exchange, and a repeat of the thrilling goal spree against Alloa would be a timely advert for the club.

The day literally began with a bang when an artillery gun at the side of the pitch marked the beginning and end of a minute's silence on Remembrance Weekend, while both sets of fans participated in a colourful card display to mark the occasion. An official attendance of 48,407 was bolstered by around 400 members of the armed forces, who were welcomed onto the pitch at half-time, with a handful of soldiers thrilling the crowd by abseiling the Govan Stand in a *Mission: Impossible*-style display that Tom Cruise would have been proud of. As well as a poppy, stitched across the breast of every Rangers player's jersey were the words "Lest We Forget".

The celebration of servicemen and women was certainly memorable; the action on the park less so once the smoke from the Howitzer had cleared and the action got underway. With Cribari and Ross Perry both unavailable, McCulloch again displayed his ability to adapt to any role with another shift in the heart of defence. Despite his rearguard duties, the former Motherwell and Wigan man still managed to net his seventeenth goal of the season when he glanced home McKay's header two minutes from half-time. Fit-again

Wallace then secured a comfortable victory when he peeled away from the six-yard box to stroke home Ian Black's free-kick. Blue Toon boss Jim McInally put the result partly down to stage fright when he said, "It's fine playing Rangers at Balmoor when it's our home game and the crowd isn't as big. To play in front of a full house at Ibrox is a massive difference."

It was hardly pulse-racing stuff but it was job done for Rangers, who just twenty-four hours later found another way to convince those hard-nosed City types to part with their cash ahead of the proposed flotation. Forget Shiels, Black, Sandaza and Templeton – Green had just pulled off the signing of the season by convincing Walter Smith to return to Rangers. It was a major coup for the chief executive, who had been trying to bring Smith on board since the former Light Blues and Scotland boss launched a takeover bid hours after Green's own consortium took control at Ibrox in June. Smith, who managed Rangers to ten league titles in two spells, joined the new regime by accepting a place on the board, along with retired Glasgow businessman Ian Hart, in the role of non-executive director. For the man widely regarded as the Godfather of Scottish football, it was an offer he couldn't refuse in the end.

The veteran boss' surprise comeback was validation in itself but there was also verbal backing for the current regime. He said, "The people who purchased the club have shown over the last few months they are serious in their intentions to rebuild Rangers and I am happy, as many other fans have done, to lend my support."

Smith stressed that such support would not extend to

him interfering in team affairs, with his one-time protégé now at the helm, adding, "Serious constructive efforts are being made to rebuild Rangers after a very difficult period in the club's history and, if I can play a part in helping that process, I am willing to do so. I must make it clear, however, that I will not be playing any role in the day-to-day running of the club or the team."

Regardless of Smith's reluctance to whip out the old tactics notebook for old time's sake, Gers fans chief Mark Dingwall felt his involvement with the board unquestionably lent credence to the new regime. He said, "It was key getting him on board because Walter had been associated with the Blue Knights and then with Jim McColl and Douglas Park, so he was obviously seen to be in a different camp to Mr Green.

"Towards the end of last season, I was lucky enough to bump into Walter at the bottom of the marble staircase. We were talking about things and I said, 'Walter, whether you want it or not, you've got responsibility because if you say something, people believe you. If you say, 'These people are okay,' then Rangers fans will believe you. They are looking to you for guidance.

"In terms of the credibility of Mr Green and his colleagues, getting Walter to sign up to the project has certainly done their credibility no harm whatsoever."

NOVEMBER 17, 2012
EAST STIRLING 2   RANGERS 6
Ochilview

There is no doubting that Smith is of the old-school variety, just like some of the venues Rangers would be gracing this season. The sort of places some people tick off on a list of football grounds in the same way others might collect Panini stickers or match-day programmes. Well, in my book, you can't call yourself a true Scottish football enthusiast unless you once paid a visit to the legendary Firs Park. Located in Firs Street in Falkirk, with the entrance squeezed between two tenement buildings, it was a proper old-fashioned football ground, like Cliftonhill or the old Boghead. It was also one of a number of venues where yours truly as a rookie freelance reporter covering matches for the *Daily Record* was turfed out of the tiny press box by some old hack claiming to have sat in the same seat for the last twenty years.

Sadly, by the time Rangers came calling East Stirlingshire had long since moved on and the place they called home for eighty-seven years was demolished in January 2012 after lying unused and derelict for almost four years. Shire bid farewell to Firs Park with a victory over Montrose in 2008, with club bosses putting the exit from their humble abode down to the costs involved in "bringing it up to scratch" to meet stringent governing body criteria. They would spend at least the next five years ground-sharing with neighbouring Stenhousemuir at Ochilview – dubbed "Lesser Firs Park" by the Shire's PA announcer, who made the move with the rest of the club.

On this particular day, after a brisk fifteen-minute walk from Larbert train station, fans milling around on Gladstone Street next to the McGowan's Highland Toffee factory were entertained by a brass band collecting for charity. As at other matches this season, a colour-coded ticket system was in operation. Rangers fans were, naturally, supplied with blue tickets, which provided access to the West Terrace. Home fans with seats in the main stand were given black tickets and those watching the action from the East Terrace had orange briefs.

Ochilview was given its name as a result of the breath-taking view of the Ochil Hills in the distance. Apparently there is an old local saying that goes, "If you can see the Ochil Hills, it's about to rain. If you can't, it's already raining." Forget a mere downpour, McCoist watched from the shelter of the tunnel as a full-blown hailstorm battered the corrugated roof of the main stand before the match. Perhaps mindful of his comments about toughening up for life in the Third Division, his players braved the elements to complete their pre-match warm-up despite the conditions. "I saw the hailstorm from the comfort of the tunnel and it did look wild," said McCoist. "If you don't fancy playing, then all of a sudden the hail-stones are coming down and you've got another reason in your mind. But my players' attitude was absolutely first class. If we give the opposition any sniff of weakness, they will come for us."

Thankfully by the time kick-off arrived the freak weather had passed and bright sunshine highlighted the stunning local scenery. It's the sort of vista that could provide a welcome distraction during a lull in play, or a particularly dull match, but there was barely a second to take in the backdrop during this clash.

David Templeton was fit again but would not be risked on another artificial surface after sustaining the injury on Annan's plastic pitch in September, but Rangers proved to have more than enough attacking threat in their arsenal without the creative winger. Referee George Salmond pointed to the spot after Shiels was felled in the box by Sean Kelly, and McCulloch did the honours from twelve yards. There was a further blow for Shire when recent recruit Phillip Zufle was sent packing for an ill-timed tackle on Kevin Kyle. Little extended the lead with a looped volley over the keeper before the home side responded when Kevin Turner connected well with Nathan Shepherd's cross.

The action continued at the same breakneck speed in the second half when Wallace drove a low shot past Grant Hay. Shire had the net bulging again when Paul Quinn – also on target with a penalty at Ibrox earlier in the campaign – converted again from the spot after McCulloch bundled over Shepherd. Despite beating Neil Alexander twice, John Coughlin's side never really looked like causing the same problems as Rangers' other hosts earlier in the season. Kyle opened his goal-scoring account for the club when he swept the ball home from close range to claim his first goal in almost two years. McCoist joked, "Even I've never had a goal drought as long as Kevin Kyle's!" Kal Naismith replaced Shiels and slotted home McKay's cut-back from the edge of the box before McCulloch struck again from the penalty spot.

Shire chairman Tony Ford had his own views on why Rangers were now collecting wins on the road and why they initially struggled. "To smaller clubs, it's a cup final, isn't it?" he said. "You maybe get 10 per cent more effort. I think the reason they didn't take to it initially was that they were just a little bit off the pace. When Ally came through to the meeting when the vote was taken, he actually apologised for what had happened. I made a point of saying to him, 'Why are you apologising? You've done nothing wrong. It's not your fault.' He came out with a comment and said, 'All I want to do is play football.' Up until that time, they had hardly done any training. If you play football as a professional and you miss pre-season training you will struggle. It's very, very difficult. It doesn't matter if you're Ronaldo or you're someone playing for East Stirlingshire, you are going to struggle because you don't get that basic level of fitness. That showed initially but once they got into their stride . . . well, we all knew that was going to kick in at some stage, it was just a matter of time. I think with the home games you get energised by the crowd, especially when you've got 50,000 people there."

Ford added, "I've struck up a nice friendship with Ally, he's a lovely guy. I actually felt quite sorry for him because all he wants to do is play on the park, it's as simple as that. As for Charles Green, I know he's taken a lot of stick but I quite like the guy. I think he's good for football. I know he comes out with a few comments here and there but he's like Mourinho. When he talks, people want to sit and listen to him. It's good for the game. People are actually talking about the Scottish game at the moment, which is fantastic."

A second win on their travels allowed Rangers to extend their lead at the top of the table to five points but a far more dramatic victory was just around the corner when the long-awaited verdict in the so-called "Big Tax

Case" was finally delivered. The findings of the First Tier Tax Tribunal were revealed in a 145-page document, which referred to key figures who gave evidence in the case as anonymous *Reservoir Dogs*-style characters, such as Mr Crimson, Mr Black and Mr Red. But in terms of entertainment value and the ability to titillate, the weighty tome was hardly *Fifty Shades of Grey* so let's stick to the key points.

The tax tribunal heard 'oldco' Rangers' appeal over a tax bill for the use of EBTs, which were in operation during Sir David Murray's stewardship. The club's argument that payments – thought to be close to £49 million – had been loans rather than wages and not subject to tax was largely accepted by two of the three judges who heard the appeal over twenty-nine days and last sat in January 2012. They determined that only some of the payments made to players through EBTs were taxable but that many of them could, as argued, be described as loans. Murray's successor, Whyte, had previously stated the liability could be as high as £75 million, including interest and penalties, for payments made from 2001-10. Murray claimed he was "duped" by Whyte, who bought the club for £1 in May 2011, paid off the £18 million bank debt on the back of future season-ticket sales and then failed to pay tax – a decision that led HMRC to force administration.

The verdict was a bit like a 2–1 win – no clean sheet but three points all the same. The victory came too late to save the 'oldco' from being wound up and did not directly affect the current Ibrox regime. However, there were immediate calls for the SPL investigation into undisclosed payments to players, which also centred on EBTs, to be scrapped. Green said, "The judgement serves to further undermine the validity of the SPL commission into the use of EBTs. As we have said all along, the SPL decision to press ahead with a commission was ill-timed and fundamentally misconceived."

McCoist added, "I would be extremely hopeful that common sense would now prevail and they would drop it. That would be the ideal situation and we could all start moving forward again."

The SPL later confirmed that the hearing would begin on January 29 after the process was delayed due to illness.

NOVEMBER 25, 2012
ELGIN CITY P   RANGERS P
Borough Briggs

Rangers could at least rely on events on the park running to schedule. Well, that was the plan anyway. Most SFL clubs had relished the opportunity to entertain the Glasgow giants and it's fair to say Elgin were pretty excited by the prospect now that their turn had come around. As well as a televised league clash on ESPN, City also had a lucrative Scottish Cup tie at Ibrox to look forward to the following week.

"Rangers in SFL Division Three has been like an injection of adrenalin," wrote chairman Graham Tatters in *Black & White*, the match-day programme. "They have brought a cash windfall to us with the live transmission of games and provided excitement that has been absent from the competition for years. No matter what anyone thinks of the circumstances that preceded their arrival here, we should welcome the team and their supporters, be thankful for the media attention and savour the moment, as it is putting the City of Elgin on the map." Elgin City were about to be placed firmly on the map and receive more media attention than they could ever have dreamt of. Just not in the way they had hoped.

The first hint that all was not right with the fixture arrived, as tends to be the case these days, via Twitter late on the Friday afternoon before the game, when a newspaper reporter tweeted that the Sunday lunchtime match was off, adding mysteriously that the post-ponement "was nothing to do with the weather". Confirmation arrived minutes later that the game had indeed been called off on safety grounds after it emerged that Elgin had sold too many tickets for their 4,500-capacity Borough Briggs home and were now unsure exactly how many briefs were in circulation. Moray Council, Grampian Police and the SFL took the joint decision to postpone the fixture in consultation with the clubs.

Match Commander Superintendent Mark Cooper said, "On Friday afternoon it came to light that tickets for Sunday's Elgin City vs Rangers fixture had been substantially oversold. After discussions with the club, it was clear that we were faced with the prospect of at least 1,100 extra fans turning up for what was an already sold out fixture."

The news sparked fury among fans, who were left out of pocket after committing to travel arrangements and booking overnight accommodation for the high noon meeting. Others, though, chose to see the funny side, pointing out that only Rangers could generate such a demand for tickets that the host club lost count of sales, at a time when empty seats in other stadia around the country was cause for concern.

"We are disappointed the match has been called off at such short notice and I know Elgin are as well," said McCoist. "I am sure this is a huge disappointment to our supporters, who have purchased match tickets and arranged travel in good faith. Elgin City have apologised to the club and we accept their apology but I feel for our fans."

However, even those Rangers fans who were inconvenienced by the call-off would have had some sympathy for the Japanese journalist who travelled 6,000 miles from Tokyo to Moray only to be confronted by an empty ground. Daisuke Nakajima spent four years in Glasgow covering Celtic matches during national hero Shunsuke Nakamura's spell at Parkhead, and he was keen to return to Scotland to report on the Rangers revival for his magazine, *Footballista*. It was only after a fourteen-hour flight, an overnight stay in Edinburgh and having already embarked on a five-hour rail journey to Elgin that he discovered the match had been postponed.

Daisuke told me, "I was so surprised that Rangers still have 50,000 supporters at Ibrox in every league game this season because Rangers belong to the Third Division. I wanted to know the reason. To find out, I thought I should go to an away game and talk with supporters. Elgin was the best place because it is very far from Glasgow. I thought supporters who would go to Elgin were very enthusiastic for Rangers. I did not expect the game would be off. It was only when I opened my newspaper after we left Edinburgh Waverley station that I discovered the game was off. It was ten minutes after the train had left from Edinburgh at 7.30 in the morning. Honestly, I could not understand what was happening. I just lost my words and thoughts."

After speaking with his editor, Daisuke decided to carry on with his journey in pursuit of what was now a much more interesting tale. He added, "I went to the stadium and got a mobile number for Elgin FC's secretary. But his mobile was switched off. I guessed journalists from *The Sun* and the *Daily Record* had phoned him thousands of times. I came across a volunteer of Elgin FC. He told me the history of the football club – but never answered the question why the game was off."

News of the wasted trip filtered back to Japan. "It was bigger news than I expected," he said. "Football games in Japan have never been called off for such a ridiculous reason."

A visit to the club shop would have provided Daisuke with some souvenirs of his unfortunate visit to Borough Briggs, with an Elgin v Rangers scarf and a "friendship" badge among the official merchandise on sale in the build-up to the game. For those with a few more quid to spare, there was also a limited edition Directors' Choice Speyside Malt, aged twenty-one years and priced at £75, to celebrate the first visit of Rangers in an SFL match. By the time football bosses handed down the punishment,

Elgin's directors were probably in need of a stiff drink.

The SFL confirmed, "The club have been ordered to pay a fine of £25,000 to the Scottish Football League, £5,000 of which will be donated to a charity chosen by Rangers FC. Elgin City FC have also been ordered to pay compensation to Rangers FC of an amount no less than the actual costs incurred by that club in the preparation and planning of this match, these expenses to be satisfactorily vouched to the board of the SFL."

There has been a long-running debate over whether the Elgin Marbles, a collection of Classical Greek sculptures, should remain in the British Museum or be returned to Athens. But there was no debating the fact that a football club had lost their own marbles, and were left counting the cost of what should have been a classic of their own.

DECEMBER

What's the Hampden Roar?

DECEMBER 2, 2012
RANGERS 3   ELGIN CITY 0
Ibrox

Anyone would think Elgin City had suffered enough humiliation for one week. They would be wrong. Not to be outdone by the person or persons who had been allowed to run amok with the ticket-printing machine, the club's fans were now getting in on the act. One excitable supporter literally became an overnight Internet sensation thanks to some unique dance moves caught on camera by Sky Sports News ahead of the Scottish Cup fourth-round tie at Ibrox. Within twenty-four hours, 100,000 people had watched the forty-four-second clip of thirty-something Jenny Bird throwing some shapes while on her own in the middle of a row of empty seats before the game.

"It's the Glasgow Ravers!" exclaimed the presenter. "Look at her go. This is some wonderful dancing from an Elgin City fan at Ibrox. I don't know what that dance is but she looks like she's having a really, really, really, REALLY good time – by herself."

Ms Bird later denied she had indulged in a generous helping of festive spirit before the game but admitted she was "mortified" by her newfound fame and had "given herself a red neck". Worst of all, she wasn't even an Elgin City fan. A Nairn County supporter, it later transpired that she made the trip to Glasgow to watch her old college pal, striker Stuart Leslie, in action. Whether his efforts on the park could compete with his friend's enthusiastic and energetic antics off it remained to be seen.

Seven days after the aborted trip to Elgin, there was finally a spectacle to witness between this pair. Kevin Kyle thought he'd claimed his first home goal for Rangers when he had the ball in the net with just over a minute gone, but his celebrations were cut short by the offside flag, a decision which appeared to be harsh. "I don't have the pace to be offside," the striker pointed out afterwards.

It was a star of the past who generated the first legitimate applause of the day when Ibrox rose in unison on the second minute to demonstrate their support for Sandy Jardine, whose battle with cancer had recently been announced. It was a scene that would be repeated at every home game while the club legend fought the illness. The assembled masses had to wait almost until half-time before they were on their feet again, their patience eventually rewarded with the opening goal. Dean Shiels had the net bulging two minutes before the break with an angled drive that fell across goalkeeper

John Gibson and nestled in the far bottom corner. Kyle finally broke his Ibrox duck after 69 minutes when he rose above everyone else in the box to connect with a Barrie McKay corner and send a stooping header beyond the grasp of Gibson. McKay was denied a goal of his own by the woodwork when his deflected effort spun off the post, before substitute Kal Naismith rounded off a comfortable win with the third goal with five minutes to go. Bright yellow football boots were not the only reason for youngster McKay catching the eye in the wide left position, and it was no real surprise to see him named Man of the Match. Just one drawback with the prize, though. "He's only seventeen so he couldn't accept the champagne," explained Kyle. "I was happy to take it for him."

It was a good day all round for the big man and also a memorable occasion for Japanese journalist Daisuke Nakajima, who finally saw a game of football. Having heard about his plight, Rangers finance director Brian Stockbridge tracked down the scribbler and invited him to the stadium for a behind-the-scenes visit before taking in the cup tie. Daisuke said, "Brian Stockbridge read my story in the newspapers and he gave me a call. He asked me to come to a tour of Ibrox. It was a great experience because I was the first Japanese who was in the trophy room. I felt the history of Rangers and how great Rangers is. Brian is such a nice guy and he gave me time for an interview. I was surprised that Sky Sports News and the newspapers knew that I was going to Ibrox. Photographers asked me to jump again and again in front of the stadium gate. I was very tired . . . I realised that the life of a celebrity is very hard!"

Daisuke had witnessed a number of Champions League nights at the stadium in the past and added, "The atmosphere of Ibrox was the same. It was great. In the second minute, supporters applauded warmly in tribute to Sandy Jardine, who is fighting cancer. It was very impressive and I love the atmosphere of Ibrox. I realised that everyone loves football and the club. The game was nice. Barrie McKay is a very talented player and I am looking forward to seeing him on the top stage in Europe. The best thing for me at Ibrox was I could see the football game finally! I was so hungry for football at that time.

"Ibrox is Ibrox. Bovril and pie were excellent! Obviously, the quality of the game was not as good as Champions League games. But the quality of the game is not the most important element for real football supporters. I think atmosphere is more important – and Ibrox has it."

Daisuke returned to Tokyo with a few tales to tell, while Elgin returned home with a split of the gate money generated by the 23,195 attendance. The lowest of the season at Ibrox this term but enough to help them pay a hefty fine.

DECEMBER 8, 2012
RANGERS 2   STIRLING ALBION 0
Ibrox

The fans were back out in force for the home tussle against their solitary conquerors in Division Three so far. The last time Rangers faced Stirling their manager

Greig McDonald missed the match to attend his own wedding. This time he gate-crashed an anniversary bash.

The visit of Albion saw Rangers celebrate 140 years since the club's formation in 1872, an occasion made even more significant for the season-record crowd of 49,913 by the turbulent events of the last twelve months. The celebrations included a card display in the stands, fireworks and a VIP guest list which comprised some of the finest players ever to pull on the Light Blue jersey. Binos fans refused to participate in the festivities, displaying a message which read, "More Like 140 Days". What looked like a hastily thrown together protest was more of a collection of A4 sheets of paper than a proper banner, but their point was loud and clear all the same as they questioned the validity of their hosts' claim to have an unbroken, glorious history following the liquidation of the old company. However, Rangers had none other than US wrestling star Hulk Hogan in their corner, who tweeted, "Glasgow Rangers 140yrs and still kicking ass. Nothing but respect."

The match was also a milestone event for Lee Wallace, making his fiftieth Rangers appearance, and sixteen-year-old Tom Walsh, who was named among the substitutes for the first time. David Templeton made his first start since his lengthy lay-off but there was no way past a stubborn Stirling side in the opening forty-five minutes, as Rangers huffed and puffed without any breakthrough.

The half-time entertainment saw around forty ex-stars welcomed onto the pitch, parading various pieces of silverware claimed over the decades. Andy Goram, Mark Hateley and Richard Gough were among the "Nine in a Row" heroes represented. Harold Davis carried the Glasgow Cup, and members of the 1972 European Cup Winners' Cup winning side in attendance included Willie Johnston, Derek Johnstone and Colin Stein. John Greig – voted the Greatest Ever Ranger – made an emotional return to Ibrox for the first time since the ill-fated Craig Whyte era. Asked by pundit Andy Gray if he was enjoying himself, Greig grumbled, "I'd prefer us to be winning."

He was duly granted his wish in the second half. Templeton broke the deadlock after an hour, driving past the goalie after a fine delivery from McKay. Stirling's hopes of a late fight-back were dealt a blow when Daly McSorley was dismissed for a second bookable offence with five minutes to go, before Gers youngster Walsh was handed his debut. Andy Little made sure of the points with a last-minute strike to avenge October's shock reverse at Forthbank.

McCoist was relieved to see his side secure the victory and avoid putting a dampener on the celebrations, confessing, "I was a little bit concerned with the way things were shaping up that we would end up with a damp squib and the result not going our way. I'm mightily relieved and pleased. The occasion was fantastic for everybody involved with the club. It was an opportunity for some great stars and players of the past – and indeed the current players – to celebrate the club's 140 years. It was also a chance to say a thank you to those fantastic supporters." The players were made well aware of the importance of the occasion and Kyle Hutton added, "The gaffer said to us beforehand that he wanted us to go out and give a good account of ourselves and get the win and do it for the fans. We did that so we are happy."

Despite failing to secure another three points against Rangers, young Stirling boss McDonald revelled in the chance to take his place in the Ibrox dugout, rather than feel overawed by the occasion. "I have to say I absolutely loved it," he said. "That's the kind of atmosphere and arena that you want to be involved in. It was great playing in front of 50,000. I was delighted for my players that they got to experience that. I was happy for my players and I was happy that we put on a decent show. I thought we knocked the ball around well. It took Rangers until the ninetieth minute to score the second goal to kill us off and we were down to ten men at that point. We hit the post when we were only 1–0 down so we certainly gave a not bad account of ourselves."

He added, "Yes, we're part time and the guys have all got jobs during the day but we've still got a fair few quality footballers, particularly some of the young guys coming through in the SFL. Rangers being in the league has brought some media focus. A lot of it is just around Rangers and, if they draw or lose a game, it's more about what went wrong with Rangers and why they didn't win that game. I feel some of the media coverage should be, 'What did Annan do well? What did Stirling Albion do well? What did Berwick do well? Who have they got in their team who could make the step up?' But I think Rangers being in the SFL has definitely brought positive media coverage of the Third Division and hopefully we will have got more supporters out of it as well."

DECEMBER 15, 2012
MONTROSE 2   RANGERS 4
Links Park

The next stop on the Rangers magical mystery tour was Montrose and only those old enough to enjoy the Beatles at the height of their fame would remember the last visit to Links Park. Six years after the "Fab Four" split up, and four years after the club's European triumph in Barcelona, the Gers travelled to the coastal resort town in August 1976 for a League Cup tie and left with a 3–0 win. Almost four decades later, Rangers were back in town and seeking a similar outcome.

In sporting terms, Montrose is generally more renowned for its golf than its football, boasting the fifth oldest course in the world, which is also a qualifying course for the Open. There's also a three-mile stretch of sandy beach, which has a Blue Flag for its Eco credentials, although it might be advisable to wait until warmer months to go for a paddle. Take a wander down to the Harbour and you'll find a bronze statue of Bamse the Norwegian Sea Dog. After his death on the dockside at Montrose in 1944, the St Bernard was buried with full military honours for his service during World War II. Gers fans may be interested to know the English translation of Bamse's name is "teddy bear".

The football ground is situated in the Mid Links area, which is roughly a fifteen-minute walk from the train station, which was also the main stop en route to Brechin on day one of this season's adventure. The Royal British Legion club is ideally situated right outside the main entrance to Links Park for those in search of a pre- or post-match pint. But hopefully the three chaps who managed to haul deck chairs onto a rooftop overlooking the park to watch the action stuck to the soft drinks for the day. The ground usually holds 3,330 fans but the attendance for this encounter was recorded as 4,205. Don't worry, the Gable Endies followed Forres Mechanics' example of obtaining a licence to increase the capacity, rather than opting for the Elgin City method of distributing tickets. Live coverage from Links Park, for the first time ever, meant the game reached an even bigger audience – and what a show it turned out to be for armchair fans, those with tickets and the three guys on the roof.

Montrose were on a six-match unbeaten run and confidence was clearly soaring as they opened the scoring after sixteen minutes, Lloyd Young dispatching a first-time volley into the bottom corner from ten yards. Rangers – decked out in the black third kit with the blue stripe design – levelled when Templeton was felled in the box by Stephen McNally and Lee McCulloch – who else? – scored the resultant penalty. In the second half Dean Shiels steered into the path of Kyle to power home, before McKay ran sixty yards and released Shiels to guide the ball into the far corner. Substitute David Gray helped himself to the pick of the bunch when he looped a stunning right-footer over Neil Alexander. Robbie Crawford had the final say at the end when he fired in off the post after McKay's effort was blocked.

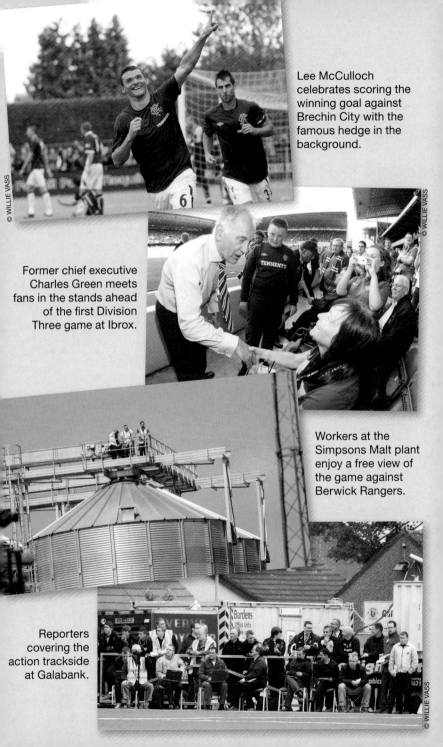

Lee McCulloch celebrates scoring the winning goal against Brechin City with the famous hedge in the background.

© WILLIE VASS

© WILLIE VASS

Former chief executive Charles Green meets fans in the stands ahead of the first Division Three game at Ibrox.

Workers at the Simpsons Malt plant enjoy a free view of the game against Berwick Rangers.

Reporters covering the action trackside at Galabank.

© WILLIE VASS

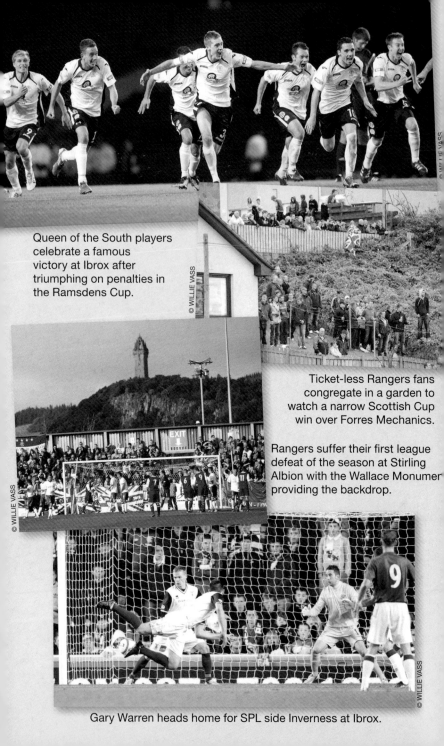

© WILLIE VASS

Queen of the South players celebrate a famous victory at Ibrox after triumphing on penalties in the Ramsdens Cup.

© WILLIE VASS

Ticket-less Rangers fans congregate in a garden to watch a narrow Scottish Cup win over Forres Mechanics.

Rangers suffer their first league defeat of the season at Stirling Albion with the Wallace Monumer providing the backdrop.

© WILLIE VASS

© WILLIE VASS

Gary Warren heads home for SPL side Inverness at Ibrox.

Soldiers with the Howitzer on the trackside on Remembrance Weekend.

© WILLIE VASS

Derek Johnstone and John Greig with the European Cup Winners' Cup during the 140th Anniversary celebrations.

© WILLIE VASS

Fans look on from a rooftop as Rangers take on Montrose at Links Park.

© WILLIE VASS

Andy Little nds the back of the net at Borough Briggs.

© WILLIE VASS

© WILLIE VASS

Clyde fans attempt a joke at the expense of their hosts at the Boxing Day match at Ibrox.

Fraser Aird demonstrates his joy at netting a late winner at Hampden.

© WILLIE VASS

Assistant referee Lorraine Clark becomes the first female to run the line at Ibrox.

David Templeton congratulates match-winner Francisco Sandaza on his goal at Peterhead.

© WILLIE VASS

Montrose striker David Gray runs towards the away fans after finding the back of the net against his boyhood heroes.

Rangers fans at the controversial Scottish Cup tie against Dundee United.

© WILLIE VASS

© WILLIE VASS

Dundee United fans wearing Craig Whyte masks at Tannadice.

David Templeton celebrates his impressive goal against Clyde.

© WILLIE VASS

© WILLIE VASS

© WILLIE VASS

Rangers fans with banners after the club retains all 54 world record titles following a probe into undisclosed payments to players.

Ally Love scores as Annan claim an historic win at Ibrox.

Rangers supporters show off an impressive pin collection at Elgin.

Kyle Hutton and the banner responding to his comments on Twitter.

© WILLIE VASS

Ally McCoist is grilled by journalists after the goalless draw at Montrose just hours before Rangers are confirmed as champions.

The statue of Bamse, the heroic Norwegian sea dog, whose name translates into English as 'Teddy Bear'.

© WILLIE VASS

Rangers fans make their feelings known at the last away game of the season against East Stirling amid off-field uncertainty.

Rangers players celebrate with the Third Division trophy at Ibrox.

Ally McCoist speaks to fans on their megaphone after Rangers are presented with the trophy in front of a sell-out crowd.

Captain Lee McCulloch lifts the Third Division trophy after the last game of the season against Berwick.

© WILLIE VASS

© WILLIE VASS

© WILLIE VASS

IRN-BRU
SCOTTISH FOOTBALL LEAGUE

CHAMPIONS 2012/13

Reflecting on his wonder strike, Gray said, "I had just come on the park and touched the ball once as part of the move. I took it first time. It was more of an instinct effort, rather than planned. It came quickly and I had to move my feet quite quickly. It was a great goal to score. But all the lads were so disappointed because we thought we would have got something out of the game."

He added, "It's been fantastic to play against Rangers. I don't think there is anyone who would say they didn't enjoy it. Even just to see full crowds at our home stadium has been great, to play in front of crowds like that. It's a lot different to what we're used to every week."

Rangers were steadily collecting goals, points and victories – but the apologies were also stacking up. The redress from Montrose followed comments in the match-day programme, which read, "Playing their first season in Division 3, The Rangers are a 'newco' of the now defunct Glasgow Rangers. Currently top of the table, they will be hoping to go on to seal the title and clinch their first silverware."

The history jibe resulted in an apologetic statement from Montrose, reading, "Due to time restraints in producing the programmes, our programme editor had accepted the pages submitted by our correspondent. However, Montrose Football Club readily accept the content within the programme must be our responsibility. At no time was the information on players or the club printed to create a slight to anyone connected with Rangers Football Club, or indeed ignore a proud and successful history, therefore Montrose Football Club very much regrets the pages included may have caused offence and unreservedly apologise to Rangers Football Club, the management, players and supporters if they felt this was the case."

Charles Green responded, "I and all our supporters were dismayed by some of the content of the match-day programme at Montrose on Saturday which was clearly intended to ridicule our club. I have spoken personally to the Chairman of Montrose and he and his fellow directors have offered Rangers an unreserved apology, which I am happy to accept. We were made extremely welcome at Montrose and the club's hospitality was fantastic, as has been our experience throughout the SFL this season."

DECEMBER 18, 2012
RANGERS 3   ANNAN ATHLETIC 0
Ibrox

The season was about to get even better. Just six months after his consortium began the process of rebuilding a club left ravaged by the previous regime, Green strode onto the Ibrox pitch ahead of the visit of Annan to announce that Rangers would be launched on the London Stock Exchange, having raised a massive £22.2 million through a share issue – including £5 million raised by fans. Green had been listed as the club's main shareholder in the share prospectus, with a stake of almost 15 per cent, which would be diluted following the flotation. Newcastle owner Mike Ashley was the third largest shareholder with 9 per cent before the issue of extra shares behind a consortium called Blue Pitch Holdings. Boss McCoist had almost a 3 per cent stake before the issue and said he planned to buy more. Addressing the fans, Green described the sums raised as "a phenomenal achievement" which would "help us rebuild the club and take us back to where we belong".

The galvanising speech had the desired affect on most of the supporters but the section of the Broomloan Front, which houses the Blue Order and the Union Bears, used Green's address to voice their dissent over plans for Ibrox naming rights to be sold off. Green had held talks with Ashley over a lucrative deal that would promote the Newcastle chief's Sports Direct retail firm, with Rangers also reportedly considering other stadium re-branding proposals. McCoist himself was "pretty open-minded" on the issue but felt fan opinion should be canvassed on any name change. Both fans' groups made their thoughts known, with messages declaring "Always Ibrox", as well as chants to a similar effect.

The pre-match drama was almost missed by Annan, whose team bus broke down outside the city on the way to the game. Any potential delay to kick-off was averted, despite the visitors arriving at the stadium later than planned. Francisco Sandaza started for the first time since sustaining his horrendous facial injury against Motherwell in September, while Kyle failed a fitness test after sustaining an ankle problem on Montrose's 3G surface. It would prove to be the amiable forward's final game for Rangers, with the injury ultimately ending his Ibrox spell prematurely some months later. However, this meeting with Annan proved to be significantly more enjoyable for Templeton than his last encounter with the

Galabankies, which had ended painfully with a swollen ankle and ligament damage.

Early pressure from the home side paid off after 29 minutes as a lovely, low drive from Templeton from just outside the area caught the opposition defence unaware. Annan were handed the chance to haul themselves back into the match amid dramatic scenes in the second half. Wallace was shown a straight red card by referee Paul Robertson, who ruled that the full-back hauled down Jack Steele in the box, while McCulloch earned himself a booking for dissent. The skipper was right to complain about the sending-off, with the dismissal later reduced to a caution on appeal. Scott Chaplain stepped up for the spot-kick but goalkeeper Alexander did well to smother on the hour mark as Rangers retained their lead.

Little handed Chaplain a lesson in finishing four minutes later when he raced onto a Templeton pass before sending an angled drive past Alex Mitchell. Templeton resumed striking duties when he added to his own tally with a low shot from twelve yards to secure a comfortable win. Chris Rea's festive classic "Driving Home for Christmas" filled the bitter cold Tuesday night air as fans filed out of the stadium, with the opposition team no doubt hoping that would indeed be the case and there would be no further transport troubles.

Anyone cynical enough to suggest that Annan probably wished they hadn't bothered finding the jump leads and making the remainder of the journey to Govan would be wrong. Chairman Henry McClelland said, "What a night it was for all of us, the fact that we got to play a game at Ibrox. There were 42,000 there on a

Tuesday night and it was a tremendous night. A couple of guys who play with us – Chris Jardine and Scott Chaplain – were both released by Rangers as seventeen- or eighteen-year-olds and, lo and behold, both of them had a chance of glory. Scott Chaplain missed the penalty to make it 1–1. And, at 0–0, Chris Jardine was one-on-one with Neil Alexander. But they took great memories from the game, as we all did."

For a midweek just days before Christmas, the attendance of 42,135 was another staggering statistic as Rangers fans continued to back their team at a stage in the campaign where some thought the novelty may have worn off. The Rangers Supporters Trust's Mark Dingwall said, "You've got parents who can now afford to take their kids to the games on a season ticket, so it's a whole new generation, a vast influx of youngsters into a support which, because of the nature of the season tickets culture, had actually become quite an ageing support.

"I see most of the games from BF1 and I think what people don't really get until you've been in there is the extreme youth of the people who are in BF1. They are having the time of their lives. The novelty of where they're playing, the cheapness of the games – they are having a high old time. That will be their memories."

He added, "The price is one part but it's a small part. The biggest thing is that people rallied around their club. It wasn't defiance, it wasn't the price. The biggest factor was that Rangers fans love their club and this was one of the few things they could actually do to demonstrate that. Putting their money into the club through their season tickets would help.

"People just keep coming. There is football at Ibrox so we're going to support our team, we're getting behind them. The club nearly died. We've been saved and we are grateful we still have a team. I think it's as simple as that. People love their team."

The game was to be Annan boss Harry Cairney's last when he stunned the Borders club by resigning just two days later to focus on his teaching job and family life. But his opposite number McCoist was already looking to the future and the potential to strengthen his squad once the transfer embargo was lifted now that there was cash in the bank.

"It was a great day off the park," he said. "The fact that the share issue is in the region of £22 million, and for the fans to chip in with roughly £5 million, I think is absolutely staggering. I think the best way I can put it is, the one thing the investors and certainly the fans deserve is for their money to be used wisely. And I would certainly hope to have an opportunity to use some of that money wisely."

Following the manager's press conference, myself and Radio Clyde's Alison Robbie were summoned to the tunnel area, where Green was waiting to offer his own thoughts on the share issue. It was my first face-to-face meeting with the charismatic chief executive and I was not quite sure what to expect from the encounter. I was not to be disappointed, as he went on to reveal that McCoist would be handed a transfer kitty of at least £10 million, that could rise to as much as £30 million, in what was a headline-friendly interview.

Green explained, "In the presentation we did when

we were selling the shares, and also in the prospectus, we said that of the £22 million, £10 million is put to one side for Ally. Of course, we can't buy players at the moment, we can't do that until January 2014. But between now and then, we'll also have another season's worth of season ticket sales so the cash position will increase. We're not saying it's £10 million and only £10 million. If Rangers fans, as we expect, come out and buy their season tickets next year, there is perhaps another £20 million there and that is a fantastic position for the manager, the club and its fans to be in. When we are allowed to go into the market, this club will take the right players and take the right action."

As far as Christmas presents go, it certainly beat socks and a selection box.

DECEMBER 22, 2012
ELGIN CITY 2   RANGERS 6
Borough Briggs

A gift was also awaiting Green when he arrived in Elgin for Rangers' rearranged fixture. A presentation took place in the boardroom before the match, where the chief executive was handed a twenty-one-year-old bottle of whisky, and apologies were made for the ticket fiasco which led to this encounter taking place later than planned.

Two days earlier chairman Graham Tatters faced an SFA disciplinary hearing, where he was found guilty of "not acting in the best interests of Association football by knowingly distributing tickets in excess of the maximum capacity of the ground at which the match was scheduled to take place". He was fined £5,000, with £1,000 to be paid within thirty days and the rest suspended until the end of the season. Tatters revealed he almost quit over the debacle but was talked round by his wife and family.

Again, the Radio Clyde team – this time Gordon Duncan and Clyde boss Jim Duffy – came to the rescue with a lift to Elgin. With a Third Division manager in the car for such a long journey, it seemed an ideal opportunity to find out Duffy's thoughts on Rangers joining the bottom division.

"I think the word 'stunned' sums it up," he admitted. "When you grow up in Glasgow and you spend all your life involved in football, from playing it as a kid to working within it, I don't think you would ever imagine or envisage that a club the size of Rangers could find themselves in the situation they did. February 14, 2012, when Rangers went into administration, was a day I don't think anyone could ever have dreamt would happen. In the summer, for Rangers to be placed in the Third Division was a surreal scenario. That's the best way I can describe it. It was really quite surreal."

I asked him how much the rest of the clubs in Division Three have benefited from the presence of Rangers so far.

Duffy said, "If you're looking for any good that has come out of it, other than the survival of Rangers, which is the most important thing, it's been a financial lifeline to a number of small clubs. There is no question about that. The huge Rangers travelling support has pretty much guaranteed full houses at every away game and that has been a huge bonus to all the clubs.

"As far as the football side has been concerned, I think it's been an education for most of us. We are playing against players who are considerably better, who are full-time, with the resources Rangers have. In comparison to the rest of the Third Division, it's just night and day. It's been an education for a number of players, for a lot of the younger players, and it shows how far they have to go if they want to play at a higher level.

"It has been exciting and it's the game that everybody looks forward to. It's THE game of the season every time you play against Rangers, especially at home when it's a full house, which is something you just don't get these days, unless you draw Rangers or Celtic in the cup."

Strangely enough, the official attendance at Borough Briggs this time around was several hundred below capacity but it was a clash that proved to be well worth the wait. Piper Garey Stewart played the teams onto the park, having warmed up with a couple of numbers beforehand. The traditional Scottish tunes added to the sense of occasion but may not have been appreciated quite so much by those who enjoyed one too many Christmas sherries in local nightspot Joanna's the night before.

"It's fish-and-chip paper as far as I'm concerned now," was McCoist's view of the original postponement. And now that they finally had the chance to go head-to-head in the top of the table tussle, both sides set about trying to make fresh headlines. It was "blink and you'll miss it" stuff, with almost every attempt on goal ending up in the back of the net.

Rangers drew first blood after five minutes when

Little collected a neat pass through the middle from Templeton, before rounding goalkeeper Gibson and picking his spot. Elgin were back on level terms after the ball broke for Daniel Moore, and he sent an impressive curling effort past the reach of Alexander. Little and Templeton linked up well again as Rangers restored their lead. The winger's cut-back found Little and a simple tap-in was all that was required from the Northern Ireland international. Again, the home side responded positively with a goal of their own. Chris Hegarty was booked for a foul on David Niven on the edge of the box and Mark Nicolson dispatched a superb swerving free-kick into the top corner. There was more to come before the interval. Little collected from Hutton before supplying the cross for McCulloch to hammer home in off the crossbar. The skipper – back in a forward role after a recent spell in defence – was on target again when he raced onto a Templeton ball and fired across the goalkeeper on the hour mark. Young Lewis Macleod added his name to the score sheet with a powerful, low strike from just inside the box. Hutton then earned himself a thumbs-up from the gaffer when he claimed his first Rangers goal, before Alexander denied Moore from the penalty spot after Hutton brought down Leslie.

Little now had an impressive thirteen goals for the campaign so far, despite a spell on the sidelines with a foot injury, but still trailed McCulloch, who was on twenty-two strikes. But he claimed games rather than goals was his motivation and denied any rivalry with McCulloch in the scoring charts. "I said at the start of the season that all I wanted to do was play in every single game," he said. "That was my main aim. I'm delighted when I score and that's a big part of my game. The gaffer keeps telling me to try to get goals. But it's not a matter of catching Lee. He's been on fire, even at the back he was still scoring a couple of penalties. Fair play to him but it's not that I'm trying to catch him. I want to score as many as I can and just do my bit for the team."

The post-match press conference took place in the social club, where Elgin players snacked on pizza and sandwiches after the game. While waiting for his own turn to speak to the media, Templeton received an unusual request from a couple of his opponents: to have his photo taken with them. "It was a bit strange, that's the first time it has ever happened," laughed the former Hearts man. "Some of these boys might support Rangers and they don't get to play against us that often. It was a weird feeling and I didn't expect it at all but it was good at the same time that the players want a picture with you. When you're playing in the game, it's not like that at all. They want to do well for themselves. It's only afterwards you can be friendly again."

The journey back home proved to be just as adventurous, with a fallen tree blocking the main road south and others swaying dangerously in strong winds and threatening to come down on top of car roofs. A supporters bus and the team bus were also trapped for a good forty-five minutes before we were informed of a back road that would take us through Grantown-on-Spey and back on track towards Glasgow. A weak, narrow bridge meant the alternative route was not an option for the larger coaches, which was probably just as well as the Rangers entourage may not have appreciated a detour which took them past Castle Grant – the Scottish residence of none other than Craig Whyte. At least when they did finally make it back to Ibrox, they returned with another three points from a potentially hazardous away clash. The road out of Elgin may have been difficult for Rangers to manoeuvre but it would appear nothing was going to block their route out of the Third Division.

DECEMBER 26, 2012
RANGERS 3   CLYDE 0
Ibrox

As well as the consortiums fronted by Green and Walter Smith, other interested parties had flirted with the idea of a Rangers takeover before the deal was struck with Green's group in June. Bill Ng was a Singaporean businessman, who was described both as "a millionaire" and "a life-long Gers fan". The owner of Hougang United, Ng was said to have been a fan of Rangers since witnessing their European triumph as a boy in 1972. Then an article surfaced from around the time of his Hougang takeover, where he was quoted as saying he had no real interest in football and didn't even know the offside rule. Another overseas contender was American Bill Miller, a Georgian towing truck tycoon. The sixty-five-year-old drove a Harley-Davidson and his missus was a one-time US beauty queen. Miller made slightly more progress and was named preferred bidder for all of five days before he, too, dropped his interest. Then there were the Blue Knights, fronted by former Ibrox director

Paul Murray. There were never any doubts about his credentials as a Rangers man, or fears over the group's motives for the takeover bid. In short, they were the people's choice. They latterly joined forces with Sale Sharks owner – and Graeme Souness' mate – Brian Kennedy but were unable to agree a deal with the administrators.

Months later, as Rangers were preparing for the visit of Clyde in a Boxing Day encounter, news emerged of another interested party. And the one we knew nothing about at the time was arguably the most intriguing of them all. Celebrity chef Gordon Ramsay revealed he had been in secret talks to buy Rangers when his company discussed investing in a consortium that wanted to purchase the club and start from scratch south of the border, before working their way to the top of the English game. A life-long Gers fan, the *Hell's Kitchen* star once trained with Rangers and featured in a testimonial match as a trialist before injury ended any hopes of a football career. Just as his dreams of being a Rangers player failed to materialise, so too did any plans to own the club, with the Green consortium completing the purchase of Ramsay's boyhood heroes. It was not the last time a move to England would be mooted this season, with Green and Ramsay sharing more than a reputation for being shrewd businessmen who are unafraid to express an opinion.

For the time being, Rangers were going nowhere, with Clyde providing the opposition for the last home match of the year. Inspired by Stirling fans before them, the Bully Wee faithful displayed a sign wishing Rangers

"Happy First Christmas", pointedly ignoring the massive signage across the middle of the Govan Rear, which lists major honours garnered over the years. Included in the list of triumphs are the nine consecutive championships won. Rangers were about to achieve another "Nine in a Row" – successive games won in Division Three – as they edged closer to another title.

Templeton stole the show, setting up the opener when his pass was collected by the overlapping Wallace, who slotted between the legs of Jamie Barclay. Not to be outdone, Templeton produced one of the contenders for goal of the season with a wonderful curling effort that left the goalkeeper grasping at fresh air. "It was a magic goal," said McCoist. "It just came back onto his right foot and he slewed it into the top corner. It was a wonderful finish." Shiels had replaced the injured Little and he wrapped up the points when he picked up the ball with his back to goal, before turning and shooting into the far corner from fifteen yards.

I was interested to know how "the Davie Cooper factor" was affecting Templeton now that he was a Rangers player and whether having such a famous namesake was proving to be a burden in terms of expectations? He told me, "He was obviously a massive player while he was here and fans still absolutely love him. It kind of helped me in a way, I think the fans took to me straight away and maybe it was because of the name. It's something that did help me and I had them on my side straight away. I felt like I could play better, hearing them take to me.

"It helped me but I wanted to get it out there that I

didn't want to be compared because it's obviously a tough thing to live up to. I wanted to make sure they knew me for David Templeton rather than Davie Cooper."

Whether an SFL championship should be regarded as the 55th title had been hotly debated among Rangers fans. Regardless, the destination of the flag was not in doubt after moving 12 points clear in pole position. McCoist said, "Looking back, I still think a big turning point in terms of our season was winning our first away game against Clyde. It got us a little bit of confidence away from home. The home performances and results have certainly been good but I've been equally as happy in recent weeks with the results away from home. I hope we do run away with the title, but we have to earn it. There's still a long, long way to go."

Clyde boss Duffy had no complaints about the efforts of his players, none of whom had ever played at Ibrox before. He said, "It was a new experience for all of the players. We trained on Christmas Eve and after the training session I was just talking to the players about the arrangements to go to Ibrox. I asked if anyone had played at Ibrox before and not one player had played at Ibrox, even as a youth player. One of the players, David Marsh, said, 'Aye, gaffer, I've played at Ibrox but not Ibrox Stadium – just the artificial pitch across the road from it.'

"In my mind, I was thinking it was going to be daunting. Not only had they not played at Ibrox before but it was going to be packed because it was a Boxing Day game. I was a bit apprehensive about how the players would handle it, truth be told, because you can go there with good teams and lose heavily. So, to go there not having set foot on the pitch before, not having had a look at the surroundings before, it could overwhelm you. There have been better players than I've got at Clyde, full-time players, who have been overwhelmed by the atmosphere and the fear factor of Ibrox.

"It was always going to be a tough encounter. For the first twenty minutes, I was absolutely delighted with the players. They seemed to revel in it, they settled down and they played all right for the first twenty minutes. From that perspective, I was actually quite pleased with how the players handled it because it was a daunting experience. Although Rangers won comprehensively in the end, it took two exceptional goals to give them a foothold in the game and, all in all, I was quite pleased with how our players handled the game."

DECEMBER 29, 2012
QUEEN'S PARK 0   RANGERS 1
Hampden Park

Rangers' last visit to the national stadium saw Nikica Jelavić grab an extra-time winner to defeat Celtic in the League Cup final in March 2011, one of numerous prizes claimed at the Mount Florida venue. Now, for the first time since November 1957, they were set to travel to Hampden on league business to face Queen's Park.

Goals from Sammy Baird, Don Kichenbrand, Johnny Hubbard (one of the spot-kicks which earned him the nickname "The Penalty King") and Billy Simpson secured a 4–2 win for the visitors in front of 30,824 fans.

Scot Symon was manager that day, with the two men in the opposition dugouts for the 2012 meeting not even born the last time the clubs met in a league fixture at the stadium. McCoist and Spiders boss Gardner Speirs used to share a room when they were in the Scotland youth squads together; now they were about to share a little piece of history as managers.

For the first time ever, television cameras were at Hampden to cover a Queen's Park game live, although they do have the distinction of being the first ever Scottish club to appear on the box. The BBC screened their 2–0 friendly victory over London amateur side Walthamstow Avenue in the capital back in 1951. An impressive achievement at a time when a lot of people didn't even own a television set. A far larger audience was expected to tune in this time, while plenty flocked to the national stadium to witness the match first-hand. The visit of Berwick Rangers was watched by 487 souls, while the visit of Glasgow Rangers attracted a crowd of 30,117. Not bad considering the North Stand was closed for preliminary work ahead of the 2014 Commonwealth Games. A pipe band and cheerleaders braved the howling wind and lashing rain to entertain those in the stands, with one home fan commenting, "Aye, you don't usually see aw' this carry oan for a Queen's gemme."

Rangers made two enforced changes from the side that defeated Clyde. Little was sidelined through injury, while Macleod revealed on Twitter before kick-off that he was ill with a virus, meaning he was absent for the first time this season. Ian Black and Crawford plugged the gaps. Queen's had given Rangers a tough match at

Ibrox in October and there was nothing amateur about this performance either, which was purely professional from the hosts. McCoist's men were toiling to break down the Queen's Park resolve, but the job should have been made simpler when the home side were reduced to ten men when James Brough picked up a second caution for a foul on Templeton after 56 minutes.

Just when Rangers appeared to have conquered their problems away from home, it was a familiar venue, and the scene of so many past triumphs, where their winning streak looked set to come to an end. The clock on the big screen clicked onto ninety, the fourth official's board showed three minutes added time and the Spiders were preparing to celebrate a hard-earned point. Then Fraser Aird struck. The Canadian-born teenager came off the bench to replace Black after a month out of action with a fractured thumb. But there was nothing wrong with the seventeen-year-old's right peg when he released a shot from just outside the area that squeezed past several bodies in the box and nestled in the bottom corner.

"It was my first goal for the senior team and nothing can compare to that goal," said Aird. "To be honest, I thought I took my touch too far. All I saw was the post and I just curled it and it happened to go in. It was a dream come true. It was unbelievable, one of the best feelings of my life. I'd say it was better than my debut, to be honest." He added, "All the family were back home in Toronto watching the game. My dad has actually been sick for the last couple of games but I told him I was on the bench so I'm sure he got out of his bed to watch the game. He'll be glad that he did."

As far as McCoist was concerned, Aird's strike was right up there with that Jelavić League Cup final winner. He said, "It's bizarre, really, but I think I probably celebrated this goal as much as I did that one. It was a really hard-fought three points. It shows you the difference in the teams and it shows you how far we've got to get back to, when you look at the personnel that played in that particular game. But the boys who were representing Rangers in this game kept going."

For Queen's Park, the late strike was like a kick in the guts, summed up by the match report on the club's website: "As a game of football, it was far from a classic. As a heartbreaker, it was right up there with the best/worst of them for Queen's Park fans. The despair in the Queen's camp was palpable; the relief in the Rangers ranks was equally clear."

For Rangers, the win allowed them to bring down the curtain on their *annus horribilis* and look to 2013 with an optimism that would have seemed unlikely just six months earlier.

JANUARY

Conference Call

JANUARY 2, 2013
ANNAN ATHLETIC 1   RANGERS 3
Galabank

For football fans in the West of Scotland, the New Year period has always been about more than just Big Ben, a few halves and nursing a hangover after the excesses of Hogmanay. Traditionally, it has also been a time to revisit old rivalries with the neighbours across the other side of the city. But no SPL football for Rangers this season meant no chance of kicking off 2013 with what would have been one of the most hotly-anticipated matches on the fixture card – the New Year's Old Firm derby. This time, Celtic were set to entertain Motherwell, while Rangers would "first-foot" Annan instead.

The first-footer usually brings gifts, such as a coin, bread, salt, coal or a drink, which is usually whisky. The offerings represent prosperity, food, flavour, warmth and good cheer. Rangers' presence in the bottom tier had already seen them provide prosperity to the Third

Division clubs, and their local communities as a whole, while the last visit to Galabank also saw them inadvertently deliver good cheer to Annan thanks to the result. Reflecting on the visit to the Dumfries and Galloway town in September, Ally McCoist had enjoyed the warm hospitality on offer but was keen to avoid a repeat of the goalless stalemate on this January 2 visit. He recalled, "Annan was the one for me. Getting off the bus there was absolutely brilliant. One minute we were in a housing estate, we took a left turn, and then we were at the stadium. Once I got over the shock, I had a wee smile. If that's how it made me feel, you better believe the boys were feeling like that as well.

"But what a welcome we got. Their chairman is fantastic, what a boy he is. He was giving me a tour of the social club and I had to say, 'I'll need to go in and give my talk to the team.' He said, 'You can do that later, come in and meet the boys.' He did it in the nicest possible way and they were brilliant at Annan, so friendly.

"But they gave us arguably the toughest game we've had all season. We lost at Stirling Albion but I've watched that game twice and we should have scored about ten. At Annan we didn't play and didn't create anything. It was a real disappointment but they played well. So, we want to go down there and do a lot better than we did last time."

In the opposing dugout this time was Euan Brydson, the Annan No.2 who had stepped up to the role of caretaker boss following Harry Cairney's surprise departure. He was hoping to land the job on a permanent basis and knew a positive result against the might of Rangers would make one heck of an addition to his CV. If the visit of the Glasgow giants was effectively a job interview, it was taking place in front of thousands of spectators across the Continent, with the ESPN cameras beaming action live from Galabank for the first time ever.

"It was tremendous for the club to be broadcast all over Europe," said Annan chief McClelland. "We had commentators from France, Sweden, Norway, Switzerland, Germany – they came from everywhere. It was just a great day."

Skipper Lee McCulloch missed out with an ankle problem, while Emílson Cribari, who recently returned from injury, was not risked on the artificial surface and Barrie McKay dropped to the bench. Darren Cole was added at right-back, Francisco Sandaza started as a lone central striker and Andy Little came in on the right flank. The difference between this outing and Cole's last start for Rangers – a 1–1 draw against Bursaspor in a Champions League group game in Turkey in December 2010 – could not be more stark. Unfortunately for the young defender, his involvement in this match was cut short when he was carried off early in the second half with an ankle injury. Cole would require surgery to resolve the problem, ending any hopes of featuring again this season.

The return to Galabank was a far happier experience for David Templeton though, with the pain of ankle ligament damage sustained at the same venue now just a distant memory, as he opened the scoring in odd circumstances. Templeton, who had since modified his footwear for non-grass surfaces, retrieved the ball on the left wing and sliced a left-footed cross that beat Alex Mitchell and nestled in the far corner. Annan levelled in similar circumstances when Ally Love delivered a cross from near the touchline that sailed over Neil Alexander's head, before Rangers restored their lead when Robbie Crawford shot into the bottom corner from twelve yards. Templeton then ensured the points when he completed a bizarre double as his twenty-five-yard strike took a major deflection off Harry Monaghan and flew high into the net.

The hosts were left empty-handed on this occasion, as an eleventh consecutive league victory saw Rangers strengthen their bid for the title. McClelland backed McCoist's men to gradually leave the lower leagues behind, as they sealed a rapid return to the upper echelon of Scottish football, but he had savoured every moment of their two opportunities to entertain his boyhood heroes. He said, "I can only tell you what it was like for Annan but the whole atmosphere was tremendous when Rangers came to town. There wasn't any big-time Billy status. The banter we got with the fans was really good.

"We've had a great experience and I don't know if it will ever happen again in the future because there is no doubt that Rangers will steadily grow and theirs will be a fast-track growth. Other clubs like ourselves are here for the long haul and our progress will be in small steps, that will always be affordable, sustainable and what we can manage. That's the way we will continue to survive but Rangers will go from strength to strength as they go back up the leagues to where they should be."

JANUARY 5, 2013
RANGERS 1   ELGIN CITY 1
Ibrox

As Rangers' own first-footers, the directors of Elgin City were invited to participate in the traditional Loving Cup toast to the Queen, which takes place before the first game at Ibrox every New Year. The Loving Cup came into the club's possession in 1937 when Rangers travelled to Stoke City's Victoria Ground to play a match in aid of the Holditch Colliery Disaster Relief Fund. The 0–0 draw raised £2,000 for the dependents of the victims of the disaster, which saw thirty miners lose their lives and eight injured due to a fire. As a token of appreciation, Stoke chairman Sir Francis Joseph gifted Rangers his own personal Loving Cup. One of only thirty cast from a special mould, the ornate vessel was commissioned to commemorate the coronation of King George VI. Joseph's only request when handing the Cup over to Rangers was that a toast to the health of the reigning monarch be carried out ahead of the first home match every New Year. As well as Rangers, Stoke City, Everton and Grimsby Town still carry out a similar ceremony.

This particular time of year, of course, also stirred memories of absent friends as thoughts turned to the sixty-six supporters who attended a football match and never returned home. Wreaths were laid at the foot of the John Greig statue and a minute's silence was observed ahead of kick-off to mark the anniversary of the 1971 Ibrox Disaster.

Once the match was under way, Rangers set about trying to add to the fourteen goals scored against Elgin in the three previous meetings between the clubs this season. They were aided by the return of McCulloch and Cribari to the starting line-up, while Macleod was also added to the side after missing the last two games with a virus. The young midfielder duly supplied the opening goal with just nine minutes on the clock, with a little bit of help from the skipper. McCulloch won the ball in the middle of the park before releasing Macleod into the box and he coolly dispatched a low shot past Joe Malin into the back of the net.

Those waiting to be entertained with more goals and expecting an onslaught to follow were sorely disappointed. For all of Rangers' possession, there was a real lack of tempo to their play. With the SPL sides currently indulging in a winter break, it was almost as if they had decided to join their former top-flight colleagues in having a rest themselves. Elgin's own task was made more difficult when Paul Harkins was sent for an early bath just before half-time for a badly-timed tackle on Ian Black. The midfielder was left on the deck with a torn boot but, despite the damaged footwear, both managers agreed the dismissal was hard on the City player. "I'd need to look at it again but my initial reaction was it was a harsh red card," said McCoist. Elgin boss Ross Jack felt referee John Beaton called the incident wrong, insisting, "I thought it was a good fifty-fifty tackle. I didn't think it merited a sending-off, probably a booking at most."

Even the numerical advantage failed to aid Rangers' cause as they struggled to put the game to bed. But, just when they thought they had held on for the points, their visitors struck with two minutes to go to claim one of the most bizarre goals of the campaign. Stuart Leslie flicked on Daniel Moore's free-kick, followed by a touch from Jamie Duff, which was blocked by Neil Alexander. But the goalkeeper's attempts at gathering resulted in a strange juggling act before he fumbled the ball into his own net. The Gers No.1 hauled his jersey over his face but could not hide from the embarrassment of the late blunder. Ironically, the front cover of the match-day programme featured a grinning Alexander surrounded by a pile of footballs but he was not smiling after failing to adequately deal with one rogue ball into the box.

Any fans off the booze in a bid to dry out in January after the festive period were back on the boos at full-time as Elgin became the only SFL3 side to take points from Rangers at Ibrox so far. However, McCoist backed Alexander to recover quickly from the embarrassing error. "I've seen the goal a good few times," he said. "He knows he made a mistake but he's been in the game long enough to handle situations like that. Goalkeepers make mistakes and everybody sees them and invariably they cost a goal. Other boys make mistakes and can get away with them. Neil is a big enough boy to handle it."

Black added, "He's disappointed. We are not going to kick him when he's down. We will pick him up. It's a team game and we are all in it together. The big man will be fine and we will look forward to the next game."

The afternoon proved to be even more painful for defender Ross Perry, who was forced to withdraw from the action with a suspected broken nose. But he took to Twitter to ease fears over the injury, tweeting, "I've prob looked better but hopefully just bad swelling. Nothing feels broken. I'll just look like a panda for a wee while. Training Monday!"

JANUARY 12, 2013
RANGERS 4   BERWICK RANGERS 2
Ibrox

Despite the setback against Elgin, Rangers remained well on course to win promotion to the Second Division – or did they? An agreement in principle between the SPL and the SFL to a restructuring plan, that would see the organisations merge in a 12-12-18 structure, had just thrown a major spanner in the works for the league leaders. If rubber-stamped for the coming season, the new format would mean a further year in the bottom tier of Scottish football regardless of any title success, albeit with the potential time frame for a return to the top flight remaining the same.

Charles Green did not take the news well. New Director of Communications James Traynor had already described the plans as "ridiculous" and an "abomination". Green went a step further by threatening to quit Scottish football altogether. He told RangersTV, "I haven't read anything other than what is in the press and, if that is what we have sat here eagerly awaiting to transform Scottish football, my advice to the board of Rangers is the quicker we can leave Scottish football the better. I can't see anything that is going to transform the finances, the status or the excitement."

According to Green, the remainder of Rangers' season would be rendered meaningless if the proposals were accepted. He added, "If this does happen what is the point of us finishing the season? Why should we send players out to get broken noses – like Ross Perry last week – or have players getting surgery when no one can get promoted and no one can get relegated? We might as well have a winter break now till next August. I can't see any point in carrying on with meaningless matches. In what league do you win a division and then end up playing the same teams again the following season? There is no meaning to it, in reality."

Green conceded that Rangers were short of alternatives in Scotland but pointed to attempts for cross-border leagues to be introduced elsewhere, with Standard Liege recently revealing they will ask to join France's Ligue 1 if a new Belgian-Dutch league is not created. If such an argument appeared almost tame by Green's standards, there was no need to worry, he had another ace up his sleeve. The Gers chief also threatened to use sex discrimination laws to sue UEFA if they tried to block moves to join a cross-border league, claiming he already had precedent on his side after the governing body sanctioned a professional women's league in Belgium and Holland. The Gordon Ramsay plan to take Rangers to the Conference and then progress through the English leagues was an idea that Green was definitely thinking of re-heating.

The debate was sparked just as Rangers were about to host an English-based club in league competition for the first time. And there was another first for the visit of Berwick Rangers, in the shape of a female assistant referee at Ibrox, with Lorraine Clark tasked with running the line. The previous weekend she had refereed Hill of Beath's game against Bonnyrigg Rose in front of a crowd of 200 at Keir's Park – now she was under pressure to perform in front of 44,976 punters. Another female ref, Morag Pirie, once hit the headlines when then Albion Rovers manager Peter Hetherston commented that she should stay at home "making her man's tea". Ten years on, Clark at least knew she had the Rangers hierarchy on side now that Green had made it clear he was a big fan of sexual equality. And a top-notch display by the match official meant the fans had nothing to complain about either.

Little stole the show instead. The striker was on the score sheet when Rangers were fortunate to escape with a draw at Shielfield earlier in the season and he was on top form with a hat-trick against the Wee Rangers at Ibrox. Sandaza did well to force his way into the congested box, but was unable to produce a clean shot and the ball fell for Little to stab over the line from an acute angle at close range. He added to his early strike two minutes after the restart by volleying home a Templeton cross, before the winger claimed a goal of his own thanks to an acrobatic volley that left Ian McCaldon with no chance. Ross Gray pulled a goal back for visitors, lashing home moments after being thrown into the action. Fraser McLaren then dispatched a bullet header into the back of the net from a Lee Currie cross to claim his second goal of the season against Rangers. But the day – and the match ball – belonged to Little when he completed his treble with a cool finish from the edge of the box. The striker confessed afterwards that securing a hat-trick had eased a guilty conscience over being at fault for one of the Berwick goals. He said, "I was really keen to get back among the goals. I'd gone off the trail a little bit so I was delighted to get a few goals. Just to keep playing is great for me. I was probably the most happy with the third, just to get the hat-trick. I absolutely love it when I get on the score sheet and to score in front of all those fans is incredible. To get three goals was extra special, especially after it went to 3–2, it was important that we got that goal. I felt I was at fault myself for their second goal so I felt it was up to me to try to get us out of it."

On a day when goals appeared to come easily for the Northern Irishman, Little had some sympathy for team-mate Sandaza, who did everything except put the ball in the net. He added, "It was great that the fans really seemed to get behind him, I think they appreciate that he's working really, really hard. He's just been so unfortunate not to get a goal. You could say he maybe played better than me and didn't get the goals and that's just unlucky. But he understands that it's a team game and he's happy to do that shift, so that's great."

JANUARY 20, 2013
PETERHEAD 0   RANGERS 1
Balmoor

Green's Conference call, having split opinion north of the border, had been heard loud and clear by clubs in England. Previous musings about the Old Firm joining the Premier League had always been met with staunch opposition from those within the corridors of power, as well as top-flight club chiefs. However, the lower end of the English leagues appeared to be more open to the idea of the Rangers cash-cow joining their ranks. Conference chairman Brian Lee refused to rule out the possibility of the Glasgow club becoming future members of the Blue Square Bet Premier. While aware that any attempts by Rangers to switch south of the border would be met by a number of obstacles, he claimed such problems were "not insurmountable" before adding, "Where there is a will, there is a way."

McCoist was unconvinced by talk of a dramatic exit from Scotland, insisting, "We will just wait and see what happens. I take a lot of it with a pinch of salt because doors get closed in your face and other ones are half-open and other ones open up. Until there is anything concrete, I wouldn't really comment on it. But it's nice to see that they're not slamming the door in our face."

The manager's own preference was to find a solution within Scottish football which suited everyone. He added, "Until anything happens, it is our target to continue to progress and re-establish ourselves within Scottish football and get back to where we want to be, which is the top league."

McCoist might have been more open to a move, providing the switch was to warmer climes, after arriving in Peterhead. His side had battled out a fortuitous 2–2 draw at a balmy Balmoor back in August; this time they were battered by a brutal North Sea wind and sub-zero temperatures. The Blue Toon proved to be aptly named as any exposed flesh took on post-mortem hues, while McCoist opted for two beanie hats and substitute Fraser

Aird wrapped himself in two coats before taking his seat on the bench. The players on the pitch were forced to contend with more than the Baltic conditions when they were confronted with what proved to be a physical, bruising encounter.

Sandaza led the line, with support from Templeton and Little on the flanks, while Black returned from suspension – and found himself hurled into an advertising hoarding following a robust challenge by Dean Cowie. Sandaza, who already had a face filled with metal thanks to a fractured cheekbone, suffered another severe blow to the puss and complained, "It was a tough game with many hard tackles. My nose may be broken but, if the ball is there to be won, I will put my head in. The referees maybe have to watch the tackles – Ian Black could have broken his arm." McCoist was not too concerned about the welfare of the midfielder though, joking, "Ian is all right but I think the hoarding will be out for three weeks!"

For all his war wounds, Spanish striker Sandaza chose a bitter afternoon in Buchan to shine when he finally ended a five-month goal drought by netting on the half-hour mark and claiming only his second Rangers goal. Goalkeeper Graeme Smith beat away a Lee Wallace shot but could not smother the ball and Sandaza reacted first to drill the only goal of the game into the net. In a match which saw five Peterhead players booked, it was ironic that referee Mike Tumilty only reached for his top pocket for the red card when Rory McAllister handled the ball and earned himself a second caution.

The Govan side had found themselves bullied in the

SFL curtain-raiser months earlier but proved they could now handle the rough and tumble of Division Three. Hulk Hogan would have been proud of his Rangers "brothers" for coming through the brawl with three points in the bag but McCoist refused to be critical of the physical exchange. He said, "I think the physicality has been taken out the game too much, so I'm not going to be hypocritical and complain about some of the tough tackling our players receive. We're all big boys, so let's get on with it. I think after the first game of the season the guys had to toughen up. They're certainly handling it better and the results we've had recently are based on a solidity and resilience, especially defensively."

Peterhead boss Jim McInally didn't want to be drawn on what he thought of the whistler's display but was happy enough to wax lyrical about the performance of his players. "I thought our attitude was brilliant and our work-rate was great," he enthused. "We started really well, and finished strongly as well, considering we're a part-time team. If the players continue to work like that, they'll do all right."

JANUARY 26, 2013
RANGERS 1   MONTROSE 1
Ibrox

Rangers' already stretched squad was depleted further when they agreed to allow Francesco Stella to quit the club after the Australian failed to force his way into McCoist's plans. The twenty-one-year-old signed on transfer deadline day, following a two-week trial, but registered only eleven minutes of first-team football, with the manager stating, "We will not stand in his way because we feel, at this stage, he wouldn't benefit the first team." Someone who had no such trouble impressing during his own playing days at Ibrox was fans' favourite Brian Laudrup, who was set to resume his relationship with Rangers in a "club ambassador" role. The great Dane, who helped the Gers to three league titles in the 1990s, visited Glasgow to hold talks with Green about the position and still looked fit enough to do a turn on the park. By the time a gruelling ninety-minute shift against Montrose came to an end, supporters were no doubt wishing that had been the case.

The clash at Ibrox was the only match in Scottish football's bottom tier to survive the severe weather conditions and an attendance of 46,273 meant more than half a million people had now come through the turnstiles to watch football at the stadium this season. McCoist made only one change from the side who won at Peterhead, with Shiels drafted into the starting line-up and Black named among the substitutes. Goalkeeper John Gibson – who had already played against Rangers for Elgin – and Martin Boyle both started for the visitors after joining on loan from Dundee. For Rangers fan David Gray, another appearance at Ibrox in front of a bumper crowd was an experience he intended to make the most of. He said, "I don't know what it was like for some of the other guys but I remember the first time we played here in September, the noise hits you like a tonne of bricks. You can see the crowd when you're coming down the tunnel and the noise just hits you. As soon as that whistle blows, it all disappears. It just turns into another game and you're concentrating on what you have to do."

Montrose looked lively early on, before Rangers were dealt a blow when Lewis Macleod went to ground following what appeared to be an innocuous challenge from Paul Watson. The youngster left the pitch on a stretcher and was replaced by Black on the half-hour mark, with knee ligament damage meaning he was unlikely to feature again for up to two months. A more promising development for the home side was the sight of the breakthrough goal, when Templeton unleashed a left-foot shot that appeared to be directed into the back of his own net by John Crawford under pressure from Little.

A hush fell over the crowd on 54 minutes for a piper's lament in memory of the supporter Robert Learmonth, who tragically lost his life at the last home game. Ibrox was silenced again for a very different reason with a couple of minutes to go when Gray stunned the majority of the crowd with a sensational thirty-yard strike that found the back of the net via the underside of the crossbar.

"It was unbelievable," he said. "As soon as I hit it, I knew it was going in the goal and I was off to the corner to celebrate. I don't know, from that distance, if you would always hit it from there in a normal game. It's hard to say whether you would or wouldn't. I had a bit of space and I took a chance. I've never heard a place go so quiet like that and I've never heard such a noise from the wee corner with our 200 or so fans. The place was silent apart from this wee bit of bedlam in the corner."

He added, "I was a season ticket holder with my dad when I was younger, until they started putting the Celtic games on a Sunday and I was playing pro-youth with Dundee United so I gave it up then. Just to walk out on that park, whether it's in a Rangers jersey or not, and to do it twice and to score, is a major dream come true. The only way it could have been slightly better was playing for Rangers but it doesn't take anything away from it that it was for Montrose.

"My phone blew up for about three days. I even got a letter from somebody who used to be a Leeds fan who randomly came to the game and who was sitting in the Montrose end. He said it was the best goal he had ever seen. All my family and people I haven't spoken to for years were all getting in touch and were pleased. My mum and dad have got the goal taped off Sky and they had a picture of it on my wall when I came back from work so they have enjoyed it as much as me."

Gray hopes high-profile matches against Rangers have helped change pre-conceived ideas about the standard of football in the Third Division. He said, "You need that wee bit of luck as well. But after what a lot of people were saying about teams and players in the Third Division, I think we've changed a lot of people's minds. The guys who are playing in the Third Division are good players and could step up to a higher level. For whatever reason, they haven't and everybody has got their own story. But it has been shown that it's not as low a level as people thought. Teams have competed against Rangers this year.

"When you go to Ibrox, or when Rangers come to

you, you're not expected to get anything. You can have a go, there is a freedom to go and play as well. I think a lot of teams have used that this year – they have a go, they've got nothing to lose. We did that at Ibrox. We defended well, we kept ourselves in the game and we still had the wee burst at the end to get the goal and get a result. To be part of that was brilliant. It's great to be part of a team that gets a result at Ibrox."

The last-gasp draw saw Rangers blow the chance to move 22 points clear at the top and McCoist was furious with the performance of his lacklustre players, who left the pitch to the sound of jeers from the home support. The Gers boss raged, "I would have booed myself. I'm probably as angry as I've ever been as manager with that performance. I'm not even interested in the wonder goal with a couple of minutes to go. You could see it coming, you could absolutely see it coming. Our overall performance was not good enough and our standard of finishing was probably worse."

Asked if his players switching off was the problem, McCoist said, "I don't know. But I tell you what, they better switch on kind of quick or they will be completely switched off. What I'm saying is, that level of performance can't, and won't, be tolerated. It seems a bit bizarre saying that when they've only had two draws in fourteen games but, at the same time, the supporters deserve a better level of performance than what they got."

Next up for Rangers was one of their toughest – and most controversial – games of the season, as they prepared to face Dundee United in a Scottish Cup tie that had been billed as a grudge match between the two sides.

FEBRUARY

Prime Minister's Question

FEBRUARY 2, 2013
DUNDEE UNITED 3   RANGERS 0
Tannadice

In a season with more twists and turns than the Big One at Blackpool Pleasure Beach, and more ups and downs than a yo-yo dieter's bathroom scales, the one constant throughout a mind-boggling campaign was the Rangers supporters. The product on the pitch was not always the best, and they were not shy in voicing their frustration when unimpressed by the entertainment offered up before them, but they were always there just the same. Filling the stands at Ibrox, taking over small towns across Scotland, backing their team. They had set world records, consistently delivered the biggest crowds in Scotland and often bettered attendances at top Premier League matches in England.

Now, for one match only, the club wanted their supporters to stay away.

Twenty-four hours after been drawn against Dundee

United in the fifth round of the Scottish Cup, Rangers took the unprecedented action of sanctioning a fans' boycott of the tie. Almost as soon as the balls were drawn out of the hat at Hampden, supporters' groups had called for a stay-away protest for what would be the first match away to SPL opposition since they were re-launched as a new company and denied entry to the top flight, the boycott the result of a range of past grievances with United and their perceived treatment of Rangers. Charles Green swiftly responded to the calls by announcing that Rangers would not accept their ticket allocation for the clash at Tannadice. "This is a unanimous decision by the board, senior management and staff at Ibrox," he said. "Everyone at this club is dismayed at the actions of certain SPL clubs, which were actively engaged in trying to harm Rangers when we were in a perilous situation, and we are acutely aware of their attitude to us. Not all clubs who voted against Rangers returning to the SPL fall into that category and, indeed, we made Motherwell very welcome when we played them at Ibrox in the League Cup competition recently.

"However, feelings remain very raw and it should be no surprise that we, as a club, feel this way. It is unsurprising too that there has been a reaction from our supporters to this particular fixture. Our only regret is that this turn of events will not assist Ally McCoist and the team in what will be a very difficult fixture. We should make clear that the club, the manager and the players all look forward to a situation where Rangers fans attend every match to support the team. The fans are our greatest asset."

United said they "did not intend to enter into a war of words with Rangers or to dignify their position by responding in kind."

The club's decision to support the stay-away protest was unique, according to Rangers historian Robert McElroy. "It's the first time I've ever known the club to back a boycott," he said. "In the last few years, the support Rangers were taking to Tannadice was reduced. Last season, you could see in photographs there were huge gaps in the Rangers support. That was because, rightly or wrongly, Dundee United were being viewed as being anti-Rangers. There was Leeds United in 1992, where Rangers wouldn't take any tickets, and Leeds wouldn't take any tickets for the game at Ibrox, but those were for different reasons. It was agreed there would be no away fans at either game. It's not really comparable. In terms of a Scottish game, this was a first for the club to actually refuse to take tickets. I think quite a few people decided not to go because the club backed it. I know some people who wouldn't have boycotted the game except for the fact that the club were saying not to go. I think that was a factor."

Arriving in Dundee for the match was an odd experience. Immediately detecting the Glaswegian accent when I gave Tannadice as my destination, the taxi driver who picked me up at the train station naturally enquired if I was a Rangers supporter heading for the game.

"I'm a journalist working at the match," I replied quickly, almost defensively. I realised I was bothered by what this stranger's opinion of me might be if he thought

I was a Rangers fan ignoring my own club's plea not to attend the match. I was confused by my own response. Did I agree with the boycott or not? I wasn't sure. The discomfiting experience made me appreciate just how torn the 365 Rangers fans who did attend the controversial tie must have felt – including the Rangers Supporters Assembly's own vice-president, Ross Blyth, who later offered his resignation after admitting his presence in the stands.

Inside the ground was just as strange. Usually the press box at the back of the main stand is surrounded by boisterous, vocal away supporters. This time, there was only a sea of empty tangerine seats, with the small pocket of Rangers fans housed in a corner of the stand over to our left. The upside was an unobstructed view of the action, which isn't always possible from our vantage point behind a packed-out away support. The downside was being denied a pre-match cup of tea and Twix after finding the shutters pulled firmly down on the nearest kiosk thanks to the lack of punters.

Speaking the day before the match, Ally McCoist refused to be critical of Rangers fans who opted to make the trip to Tannadice, saying, "We've taken a stance on it and we've already made our views clear on it, that we didn't take any tickets. It was all or nothing for me, that's my opinion. But we've got such a great support and I can understand that they want to travel all over the world to watch us, and they're proud of the fact that they don't miss any games. So I can understand the fans' disappointment and I can understand some fans wanting to go."

A mere sixteen seconds into the match, those who did

buy a ticket for the Rangers end must have been wishing
they hadn't bothered. A gigantic banner unfurled at the
last home match against Montrose declared, "Carry our
noise with the badge on your breast. Give them HELL at
Tannadice." And it was hellish all right.

Gavin Gunning's hopeful long punt was met by Jon
Daly's flick-on, and with Ross Perry and Emílson Cribari
succeeding only in clattering into each other, Johnny
Russell was able to run onto the ball and fire a low finish
past the outstretched hand of Neil Alexander. Russell,
the subject of a reported £400,000 deadline day bid by
Sheffield United – that was looking increasingly derisory
by the minute – also struck the crossbar, having glanced
a header wide of target. Daly was then given too much
space as he connected with a Willo Flood free-kick and
nodded past Alexander with 37 minutes on the clock.
Stay-away Gers fans watching from the comfort of their
living rooms at least had the option of hiding behind the
sofa. For those at the match, there was nowhere to hide
as they were mocked mercilessly by the home support.

"You're not Rangers anymore," they crowed glee-
fully. There was also a relentlessly repetitive rendition of
the Cranberries' hit "Zombie", which quickly became a
source of irritation for more than just the Rangers fans.
Some United supporters wore Craig Whyte masks, while
celebrity fan Lorraine Kelly, clearly dazzled by her team's
display, opted for rather less controversial tangerine
sunglasses.

To suggest Rangers were playing like the Third
Division team they now were in name would have been
an affront to some of their league rivals who had

impressed against the Glasgow giants this season. McCoist was without key performers, in the shape of Lewis Macleod and Lee McCulloch, but could rightly have expected more from those at his disposal, particularly several players with recent SPL experience. There was a partial resurgence from Rangers in the second half and Ian Black was just wide with a half-volley before David Templeton's low effort was saved. But the fatal blow was delivered by a fine second goal from Russell with ten minutes to go. Michael Gardyne nodded down for Daly and he played into the path of Russell to sweep into the back of the net from six yards. A loss of composure at the end saw Rangers reduced to nine men. Substitute Kal Naismith was shown a straight red card for a horrible challenge on Flood and was quickly followed to the changing room by Black, who picked up a second yellow – and then pretended to pick up the corner flag as though to aim at the United fans as he headed off the pitch.

Explaining his antics, the midfielder said, "I'm a bubbly guy, I like a bit of a laugh and I give as good as I get. If people want to criticise me for that, they need to get a life. If you've not got a sense of humour, you're a very sad person. I take a bit of stick and it's a bit of banter. They say I've got a track record but there are certain individuals who just love to stick the knife in. I'm big enough to deal with that. If you watched it, you saw their players as well pleading with the referee, so I think the people who are criticising should look at the great honesty from the opposition and that says it all."

The victory allowed new United boss Jackie

McNamara to begin his tenure on a high, as the seventh-placed Tangerines claimed their first home win since August. The result also provided confirmation that there would be no Old Firm derby for the first time in 122 years. With the exception of the two World Wars when football was halted, this would be the first season since 1890/91 when the great rivals would not meet in any competition.

Mark Dingwall of the Rangers Supporters Trust hailed the boycott as a success and denied that the lack of fans had a detrimental impact on the players on the pitch. He said, "I think it comes down to the quality of the players. Professional footballers play professionally. There have been very few occasions in my lifetime when I've been in a crowd and the crowd has been a major factor. I don't think it was a factor up there. The quality of the player pool between the two clubs was exponentially different. United had also been playing at a far higher level of football for the whole season. The only time, I would say, that Rangers have really turned in a good performance was against Motherwell. The football hasn't been great compared to what we have historically been used to."

He added, "I think the boycott worked in that it was a warning shot to other clubs who behaved in a disgraceful manner, that, in the years to come, they will be vulnerable and when Rangers fans get the chance their comeuppance will be delivered one day."

For Dingwall, the decision of Green and his board to back the boycott was another significant step forward in his relationship with the fans. He said, "If you look at the number of times that Mr Green has been prepared to go in front of fans to explain umpteenth things, whether it's private meetings or public meetings, he has gone right out of his way to take into consideration what the fans think. I think they are very aware that they are outsiders and, if they don't, it could very easily go wrong for them very quickly. Probably the boycott is the biggest example of that. There was almost a universal call, certainly from the fan organisations, for a boycott as a demonstration against Dundee United and, when they saw the force of the feeling, they went with it."

FEBRUARY 9, 2013
RANGERS 4   QUEEN'S PARK 0
Ibrox

On February 14, 2012, when Rangers were forced to call in the administrators, even legendary Scottish comedian and diehard Celtic fan Billy Connolly failed to find any humour in the situation. The "Big Yin" phoned McCoist when news of the club's perilous financial state broke and despite both being well known for their good humour, the pair couldn't come up with a joke between them to lighten the mood.

The manager recalled, "Outside the drama and concern of going into administration, people realised that it was people's livelihoods which were affected and were in jeopardy. Everybody knows Billy is a Celtic man, but why shouldn't he pick up the phone? It speaks of the level of the person more than anything. His message was, 'Keep going. There's a lot of good people at the club and you'll come back again.' As you would expect, it was fantastically positive because he's a positive guy. It might have been the only time he didn't crack a joke, but the gallows humour in here at that time was of paramount importance. It keeps you going and for the playing staff and the coaching staff it was badly needed."

Connolly has a seat for life at Celtic Park but at that time Rangers fans could not have been sure of making the same claim about Ibrox as storm clouds gathered in Govan and a major question mark was placed over the future of the club. Such was the shock generated by the demise of such a great football institution, interest in the fate of Rangers extended way beyond the Tuesday night pub quiz in the boozer on Dumbarton Road. As a contestant on *Celebrity Mastermind*, Val McDermid was asked which club had played their first Third Division game against Peterhead after demotion to Scottish football's bottom tier. As a Raith Rovers fan, with a stand named after her at Starks Park no less, the question was a doddle for the Fife author, while another hopeful on quiz show *The Chase* was also spot on when posed with a similar teaser about the Light Blues. There was no doubt about it, the fate of the fallen giants was big news.

Now, just days before Rangers prepared to mark the first anniversary of administration, the big question facing McCoist was whether or not he could steer the club back on track, following the derailment in Dundee, as they continued on the road to recovery. Rangers knew points made prizes and victory over Queen's Park would allow them to extend their lead at the summit to 22 points. McCoist made three changes from the calamitous cup outing, although with Francisco Sandaza and Perry both injured, two of those could have been seen as enforced. Anestis Argyriou made his first appearance since December and Chris Hegarty and Barrie McKay also started the top-of-the-table clash at Ibrox.

As well as the now regular occurrence of a minute of applause on two minutes for Sandy Jardine, there was also a tribute on eight minutes for troubled former Light Blues star Paul Gascoigne, as he battled alcoholism in a rehab clinic in Phoenix, Arizona. For Rangers fans, Gazza's time at Ibrox would always be remembered for the sort of outrageous talent that once saw him run almost the length of the entire pitch to score a memorable goal against Celtic, or for the cheeky Geordie humour which resulted in a caution from Dougie Smith after the player jokingly booked the ref with his own yellow card. Such genuine superstar ability might not be so prevalent within the Rangers ranks these days, but the crowd did have reason to rise to their feet a further four times against the Spiders.

Black successfully transformed himself from zero to hero in the space of seven days when he left the corner flags alone and turned his hand to scoring instead. The midfielder claimed his first Rangers goal five minutes into the second half, when McKay was released down the left flank by Lee Wallace before providing the cross for Black to volley home. The second goal followed good build-up play, which was capped off by Dean Shiels squaring to Andy Little for a simple finish from close range. Shiels had the net bulging himself when he ran onto Wallace's cut-back from the by-line to side-foot past goalkeeper Neil Parry to wrap up the points. Queen's had proven themselves to be stubborn opponents in previous encounters and Little added a further positive spin to the scoreline with a minute to go when he coolly curled past Parry after Wallace was again the provider.

The second-half performance matched anything served up by Rangers so far this season and was the perfect tonic for McCoist after watching his players turned over at Tannadice. "It was just what the doctor ordered," he admitted. "They kept going in the second half and I was very pleased with the performance and result, but the level of goal was really good as well. I've been saying for a few weeks now that we should be scoring more goals and the level was very good."

McCoist was then asked by one reporter if the last year had been the best or worst of his life. Yup, you read that correctly, had the last twelve months, possibly, by any chance, been the BEST of McCoist's life?

"Did you say best year?!" spluttered the manager. "No, with the greatest of respect, I've had better years! You've knocked me sideways there! It's possibly been the most difficult year but I wouldn't say worst year. It's certainly been the most difficult year in my working life, there is absolutely no doubt about that. We just need to put everything into perspective and we are content with where we are at the moment. Not delighted, not delirious about the whole situation, but when you look at where we were a year ago, we are content. But definitely not the best year! Double quote me on that if you want."

So, it was safe to say then that the past twelve months

hadn't been simply the best for the gaffer. And the difficulties faced by McCoist, as he almost single-handedly held Rangers together during those traumatic times, was acknowledged by Green.

Speaking on February 14, 2013 – one year on – he said, "Given the events of the last year, Ally McCoist deserves everyone's full support as he and his team continue to make the Rangers team strong again. The most outstanding feature of the last year has been Rangers fans themselves. Nothing could have prepared me for what I have seen at Ibrox and around the world. Loyalty is an overused word, but the attitude of Rangers supporters in the last twelve months to the club they love has been the true essence of loyalty and humbling to witness. Moreover, the strength of character shown by supporters has won recognition and admiration both here and internationally. Every Rangers supporter stands tall today and can look forward. We are on the way back."

FEBRUARY 16, 2013
CLYDE 1   RANGERS 4
Broadwood

It would be a few years before Green – or anyone else for that matter – would be able to enjoy the sensation of hairs standing up on the back of the neck as the Champions League anthem boomed out at Ibrox once again. But Rangers did manage to grab themselves a piece of the action this season by offering Juventus the use of their Murray Park training facilities ahead of the last 16 clash against Celtic at Parkhead. It was a move that sparked controversy, with some folk objecting to the idea of aiding foreign opposition against a fellow Scottish team in European competition. But as far as some of the Rangers players were concerned, the opportunity to watch the Italian champions in action at such close quarters might just boost their own game.

Kyle Hutton, Wallace and McCulloch had high expectations about what they could expect to witness as the *Bianconeri* prepared for the crunch match. Set-piece specialist Andrea Pirlo curling a few into the top corner? A lesson in finishing from Fabio Quagliarella? Or how about a defensive master-class from Andrea Barzagli? Forget it. Instead, the trio were left with some idea of how it feels to be Peter Odemwingie on transfer deadline day when they found themselves locked out of the Auchenhowie complex, as Juventus kept their session firmly under wraps and their tactics well away from prying eyes.

"We weren't allowed in – even our sports scientist got chucked out the gym for having a peek!" moaned Hutton. "Myself and a few of the boys wanted to watch Juve training at Murray Park. Lee Wallace, Lee McCulloch and myself were planning on heading up to watch them. But I heard they had a bit of an entourage with them so we were kept at arm's length. I enjoyed watching the game itself, they're a great team with some great players, but it would have been better to watch them train."

Celtic may have suffered a comprehensive 3–0 defeat at the hands of Juve, but the match succeeded only in whetting Hutton's appetite for a return to Europe's elite club competition. He added, "One of my first games in the Champions League was against Manchester United so I've experienced that atmosphere and watching Celtic playing Juventus made me a wee bit jealous that we're not playing in those types of games. Our aim has to be to get back up there and I'm sure if we work hard then it will happen."

For now, the midfielder would have to settle for Clyde at Broadwood. And, as Rangers returned to the scene of one of their more impressive outings this season, they proved they didn't need any help from the Italians to get the job done in Cumbernauld. The Ibrox side were unchanged following the win over Queen's Park. With McCulloch, Sandaza and Kevin Kyle all still injured, and Kal Naismith suspended, Little was again tasked with leading the line after grabbing a double against the Spiders.

The Northern Irishman needed just eight minutes to find the back of the net again against Clyde. He played the ball out to Shiels on the right before bursting into the box to collect the return pass, and all that was required was a simple finish past goalkeeper Jamie Barclay. Little grabbed his second of the day after 25 minutes, this time racing onto a Hutton pass before turning marker Iain Gray and lashing high into the net.

"Templeton has gone right off the boil recently," announced one of the reporters in the crowded press box, arms folded, shaking his head in obvious disdain. Seconds later, the former Hearts player produced a contender for goal of the season when he let loose a superb thirty-yard pile-driver that cracked off the inside of the post and over the line. The Bully Wee threw themselves a lifeline early in the second half when Stuart McColm whipped into the path of Kevin Watt, and he stabbed home at the front post. However, Templeton proved that he was, in fact, now on blistering form when he struck again with another impressive goal – and his eleventh of the season. The winger demonstrated some lovely movement as he surged into the box from the left before dispatching into the far corner from a tight angle, as the aforementioned journalist sank further into his seat. "Templeton's two strikes were absolutely fantastic goals and would have graced any level," beamed McCoist.

Strange goings-on had been known to happen in meetings between these two clubs in the past. Way back in February 1899, a penalty kick was retaken THREE times due to various infringements, including the Clyde goalkeeper crawling on all fours towards penalty taker Robert Hamilton as he prepared to take the pressure kick. The odd tactics worked and the spot-kick was eventually saved, although Rangers won 4–0 anyway. Then there was the curious incident of the dogs on the football park when two strays invaded the pitch in a 1973 encounter, which provided new meaning to the phrase, "Dugs at Shawfield". And this time? Step forward joker of the pack, Bully Wee assistant Chic Charnley.

"Coisty kept thinking there was somebody from our support behind the dugout throwing something and hitting him," explained boss Jim Duffy. "A couple of times, he was like, 'What the hell is that?' It was Chic; he was throwing Midget Gems at him. He hit him with a couple of Midget Gems on the back of the head. Ally turned around and he looked at Chic, and Chic was laughing like a schoolboy. You couldn't do that with somebody you don't have a good rapport with. But once the game starts, the Midget Gems stay in the pocket and you have to focus on the game!"

While success was sweet for McCoist, Duffy confessed that his own mood was not quite so jovial upon the full-time whistle, having ended up empty-handed against the Glasgow side once again. He added, "We've known each other for a long, long time. I played against all the Rangers staff – Coisty, Kenny McDowall and Durranty – I played against them many times and managed clubs against teams they were involved with. I've come across them from a professional side and socially we've met on a number of occasions and always got on well.

"There is a bit of banter, a bit of joking around the tunnel before the game. After the game, of course, the winning team is always going to be a bit more buoyant than the losing team, so I wouldn't say I was the same in terms of personality after the game. It doesn't matter if you're playing Rangers or not, you're always disappointed when you lose."

Rangers had arrived at Broadwood four months earlier in desperate need of an away victory. This time, they showed just how far they had come in Division Three by notching their eighth consecutive league win on the road. Green, however, wanted them to travel further still, revealing he had written to the Prime Minister in a bid to move the Ibrox club out of Scottish football.

FEBRUARY 23, 2013

BERWICK 1   RANGERS 3

Shielfield Park

As well as penning letters to No.10, Green had been busy on the blower to a number of clubs across the Continent and making further trips to the Post Office to stick some cheques in the post. GAIS, Orebro, Palermo and Rapid Vienna all confirmed payments had been received after Rangers announced they had settled all outstanding football debts. With their house in order off the pitch, the players now had the chance to put on a show in their televised clash at Berwick and show David Cameron why he should back their bid to play football south of the border on a more regular basis.

Berwick Rangers are the only English side to play in Scotland but are one of a number of football clubs around the world currently plying their trade in a different country to the one in which they are based. Those who regularly cross the border to play their football elsewhere include FC Andorra, who play in the Spanish leagues; San Marino Calcio, who compete against Italian opposition; Canadian outfits Toronto FC and Vancouver Whitecaps, who play in America's MLS; and New Zealanders Wellington Phoenix, who feature in Australia's A-League. Of most interest to Green, however, would be the Welsh-Anglo connection, with Swansea City, Cardiff City, Newport County and Wrexham amongst the Welsh clubs featuring at various levels of the promised land of the English leagues.

Six minutes into the match, Argyriou had the ball in the back of his own net after failing to deal with a Neil

Janczyk corner into the box under pressure from Darren Lavery. A small but vocal section of the Rangers support then scored an own-goal of their own by indulging in sectarian singing. The club had worked hard in recent years to eradicate offensive chanting at their football matches, a problem which had previously damaged Rangers in terms of both reputation and bank balance, after being hit with hefty fines. However, the chants at this match – which even included the unwanted return of "No Pope of Rome", a song which had long been abandoned by Rangers fans – were clear enough for broadcasters ESPN to issue an apology to their viewers. Presenter Ray Stubbs said, "We want to talk about the football but there has been some sectarian singing during the first half and we're going to contact the police and the authorities here to find out what can be done, if anything, about that."

A bit like the remains of Richard III, which had turned up in a car park in Leicester, the sectarian element within the club's support refused to remain buried firmly in the past. A Shiels penalty and a belter of a goal from Little handed Rangers the advantage heading into the break, as "Penny Arcade" crackled out of the ground's old speakers. But, by now, the more unsavoury tunes had already overshadowed the action on the park in the opening forty-five minutes. Rangers wasted no time in condemning the actions of the small band of supporters who had shamed the club. With the second half underway, my Blackberry beeped with a text message from the club's press office, stating, "The club is disappointed by certain outbursts of inappropriate singing by a section of the support at Berwick. Our fans have been excellent this season, both home and away, and we do not want to see this tarnished." Northumbria Police later confirmed two arrests were made and that video evidence would be passed on to officers from the Football Co-ordination Unit for Scotland (FoCUS) team at Strathclyde Police.

On the park, there was still a game of football to be won. Having suffered a knock to the face in the first half, Ross Perry already looked like Sylvester Stallone after going a few rounds with the big Russian in *Rocky IV*, and was forced out of the action after the break with a torn hamstring and a broken nose. It was another set-back for Rangers, who were also without fellow centre-half Emílson Cribari, who was in his sickbed with a dose of the flu. Despite a weakened Rangers rearguard, Berwick never looked like causing the same problems that earned them a well-deserved draw at the same venue earlier in the season, and, when the knockout blow was delivered, it came courtesy of an unlikely source.

Perry's replacement, Sébastien Faure, had been something of an enigma since his arrival at Ibrox in the summer, having spent almost his entire career until that point with Lyon. Having been born and raised in the French city, he came through the youth ranks at the Stade de Gerland but failed to make an appearance in Ligue 1. Injury hampered his final year in France, including a loan spell with Nantes, before he made an appearance in a 2–0 win over Alfreton Town while on trial at Leeds United. The Frenchman had largely flown under the radar so far at Rangers, partly due to his absence following hernia surgery, but was suddenly thrust into the spotlight after bagging not only his first Rangers goal, but his first goal in senior football. "Hopefully I will start more games now but that is down to the choice of the coach," said Faure. "But I am very happy with the way my first season is going here and I was very happy to score my first goal for Rangers. I am enjoying myself – this is a really good experience for me. I have signed for three years and have had a good start. I played seven games at the start of the season and then had a hernia injury. Now I am starting to play games again and hopefully I can earn a starting place in the team."

Faure celebrated his strike by planting a smacker on the badge and added, "Yes, I did kiss my jersey, it was good. Scoring was important for me."

Boss McCoist was keen to single out Little's strike for praise, as the Northern Irishman netted his fifth goal against Berwick alone this term. He said, "It was a brilliant goal, one of the best I've seen this season. The volley was sensational, it really was a top goal and it came at a great time for us." However, the manager was also forced to acknowledge the unsavoury songs within the travelling support, sighing, "I came off the park to be told the club have issued a statement. I back the club's statement 100 per cent. If there was some unsavoury chanting, they've probably let themselves down – and they've let us all down a little bit. I would be very hopeful it's an isolated incident and we can move on."

Asked if fans should be issued with a "safe song sheet", outlining what chants are and are not acceptable, McCoist replied, "If that eradicates the problem, then

I'm all for it – absolutely all for it. Anything that would move us forward and eradicate that problem would be helpful. It might seem like a drastic measure but, if it helps, then I don't have a problem with it at all. In fact, I'd encourage it." He added, "I don't have any doubts that the majority of our fans want to leave those days behind us. We will move forward, because we have got a phenomenal fan base who have been nothing short of fantastic this season. The vast majority of them know what is expected, because they are representing the club as well. It's important that they behave themselves and the club has a good image moving forward. I want them to come and sing the songs that get the Rangers team going but support them in the proper manner. That is exactly what we want. I'm very hopeful that this is just a minor hiccup."

With the Green party lobbying the PM to back the idea of cross-border leagues, the off-field action was hardy the best advert for Rangers playing in England. But the action on the park, at least, provided some decent entertainment for armchair fans on both sides of the border – once they'd hit the mute button on the remote control.

FEBRUARY 26, 2013
STIRLING 1   RANGERS 1
Forthbank

It's fair to say that Rangers' adventures in the Third Division had produced more surprises than Cilla Black in her heyday. So far, we'd had the ticket fiasco at Elgin, Walter Smith's return, Dermot Desmond admitting he missed Rangers, working Wi-Fi in Forres and a shock defeat at Stirling. And just as Rangers were preparing for a return to Forthbank, aiming to right the wrongs of that display in October, along came the biggest shock of them all when Ian Black revealed his favourite hobby. Forget wrestling with crocodiles or bare-knuckle boxing, the brawny midfielder opted for a more sedate way to pass his time away from football – confessing he was hooked on FISHING. And not even the Robson Green-style extreme stuff either. He might be in possession of more cards than your average Clintons, but Black claimed his hard-man image was all wrong. Having already described himself as just a "bubbly guy", the former painter and decorator was keen to paint an image of a chilled out character off the field, who simply possessed a desire to win on it.

"As soon as I cross that white line I'm a live wire because I've got that winning mentality," he said. "But off the field, I'm different – I like a bit of fishing. When I was at Inverness I used to go fishing two or three times a week.

"I'd go there and sit, just myself and a mate, and we wouldn't say a word for three or four hours. People find that amazing, but that's what I do. It's great. I love fishing. You wind down and you can think. It's just very relaxing. I like trout fishing. I think when people meet me and get to know me they realise I'm a totally different person to the one they thought. Don't get me wrong, I'm a winner when I go on that pitch. I've a job to do until that final whistle goes, but after the game it doesn't matter if you've been having a kick at me, I'll shake your hand and I'm happy to go for a pint. But it's my job and I have to win."

Black, like the rest of his team-mates, was hoping to reel in three points on their return to Stirling – the only Division Three ground where victory had eluded them. The league leaders started the game a massive 37 points ahead of the second-bottom Binos, with Cribari well enough to deputise for Perry and Naismith given the nod ahead of Barrie McKay. A full house of bottom-tier venues appeared to be on the cards when Shiels slotted a finely-weighted pass into the path of Little, who took one touch to round the on-rushing David Crawford before rolling the ball into the empty net after just sixteen minutes.

But there is nothing quite like a famous, historic victory for cranking up the self-belief and Stirling were never likely to roll over and simply accept defeat. They were back on level terms six minutes after the interval when Kieran McAnespie's free-kick picked out Ross Forsyth to bullet home the equaliser. At least the some-what muted Rangers fans were on their best behaviour after the events at Berwick. It was the players who were responsible for the red faces against Stirling as they trudged out of Forthbank without a win for the second time this season.

"We did excellent again at Forthbank, getting the draw," said Binos boss Greig McDonald, who was in the dugout this time. "If it wasn't for Neil Alexander's save in the last minute, we could maybe have got more out of the game, but I think a draw was probably a fair result." He added, "I said to the guys at the start of the season that on our day we are capable of beating anybody, and I included Rangers within that. Thankfully, we have done well against them. Rangers are obviously a quality side and I think it took them the first quarter of the season to adjust to the SFL, the different stadiums, the different tempo of football, the different style of football. I think we all knew, with the quality Rangers have and the budget that they've got, that they would pull away.

"But I think it's credit to the SFL that it took a bit of time to do and a few teams have got results against Rangers. It can only be a plus point for the SFL. A lot of people, before a ball had even been kicked, had written off the rest of the teams in the SFL, saying Rangers wouldn't lose a game, they would hardly lose a goal and they would be winning 5–0 or 6–0 every week. The Third Division teams, and the SFL in general, should take a bit of credit for being not quite the Neanderthals that we're painted as. We can play a bit of football and we can get results."

The 1–1 draw allowed Rangers to take another step, albeit stumbling, towards the SFL3 championship. And as they sought to add to their honours, Rangers were finally given the news they had been waiting almost a year to hear – that they would not be stripped of any of their previous 54 titles.

An SPL-appointed commission imposed a fine of £250,000 on the 'oldco' after finding the Ibrox side guilty of failing to make proper disclosure of side-letter arrangements during 2000–2011. But the club avoided the most severe sanction of losing up to five SPL titles won during the period investigated after the commission ruled Rangers "did not gain any unfair competitive advantage". Mixed with a sense of vindication was a feeling of anger, with Sir David Murray branding the whole process as a "retrospective witch hunt", while describing the unanimous decision of the commission as "satisfying". McCoist said, "As a former player, I know how hard it is to achieve success on the pitch and the suggestion that somehow Rangers sought to gain unfair advantage was deeply insulting to me and others who had worn the Rangers jersey with immense pride. I found the whole approach to this matter by the SPL utterly bizarre and misguided. Our fans will take great heart from this and hopefully now, after all that we have been through, there will be a widespread realisation that it is time to move on. Rangers have a huge amount to offer Scottish football and we have always been more than willing to do our bit for the good of the game."

The 'newco' club initially refused to recognise or co-operate with the hearing, although both 'oldco' and 'newco' were represented at the hearing in the end. Green commented, "It is abundantly clear from the ruling there was no attempt by Rangers Football Club to secure any unfair advantage or to cheat, as so many people asserted without giving any regard to the actual evidence. Every Rangers fan will be delighted that the commission refused to get carried away on this agenda. It is fair to say that there was, at one stage, a very unhealthy desire to press on with an investigation into this matter when cool heads and clear thinking was required. Instead, there was a frenzied atmosphere around Rangers caused by the club's insolvency situation.

This issue could have and should have been dealt with by the board of the SPL rather than embarking on an unnecessarily grand and expensive process. At the end of the day I am left with the impression that this has been much ado about very little and a great waste of energy, time and money."

A couple of days later, ahead of the next home match, one enterprising street vendor outside Ibrox added a brand new scarf to his collection, emblazoned with two words: Not Guilty.

MARCH

Mission: Accomplished

MARCH 2, 2013
RANGERS 3   EAST STIRLING 1
Ibrox

The SPL commission may have ruled that Rangers gained no unfair sporting advantage over their rivals on the football park, but assistant boss Kenny McDowall was more than happy to take advantage of the gaffer's response when news of the verdict broke while they were on the golf course. Ally McCoist was teeing up on the first at Dundonald when he took the phone call at 10am that informed him Rangers would retain all 54 of their titles. What followed was a round to remember.

"I had been waiting for the call and I probably wouldn't have played the first hole if the news had gone the other way," said the Gers boss, who revealed he would have quit Rangers if the club had agreed to being stripped of titles the previous summer.

"It's the first game I'd played in five months and it was one of the best days I'd had in months. I was really aware of the importance of the decision. You always hope – and think – that the right decision will be made but you never know. The best way I could sum it up is that I gave Kenny McDowall a putt on the eighteenth from five feet for a half for the game, and I've never done that in my life before. He looked at me as though I'd just come off a spacecraft!"

It had been a good week for Rangers. According to chairman Malcolm Murray, the "legal elephant" had now left the room, following the "10,000lb gorilla" his predecessor Alastair Johnston spoke of when referring to the "Big Tax Case" in April 2011. Rangers could only hope there were no more giant animals lurking in corners and waiting to cast a shadow over their ongoing recovery. For now, there was more positive news with the announcement of new sponsorship deals with Puma and Blackthorn Cider to boost the feel-good factor further. All the fans needed now was a win against East Stirling to raise a glass to.

There was a special guest in the directors' box for the clash at Ibrox, with Sandy Jardine well enough to attend a match for the first time since confirmation of his battle with cancer some months earlier. The Light Blues legend who made over 600 appearances for the club thanked fans who continued to pay tribute to him with warm and appreciative applause at every home game. He said, "It has been a difficult time for me and my family but the support I have received from the Rangers fans and staff at the club has given me a huge lift. I am looking forward to coming back to Ibrox again and I am sure it will be an emotional afternoon for me. I know the supporters have been staging their own tribute with a minute's applause in the second minute of games at Ibrox, and I have to say that is something I am eternally grateful for and will never ever forget."

McCoist added, "Everybody was delighted and visibly moved to see him back. I thought he was looking brilliant. He came in for a cup of tea before the game. He obviously looked a little bit weaker than normal after what he's been through, but I think he's looking remarkable. He's still got a good bit to go but, having spoken to him, if anybody is ready for the challenge and the fight ahead it's Sandy Jardine."

There was also the welcome return of Lee McCulloch, who was back in action after seven weeks on the sidelines through injury, and who started up front alongside Andy Little. The pair was embroiled in a personal race to finish as Rangers' top scorer, but for the second time this season it was the Shire who struck first at Ibrox. Andrew Stirling, taking a break from a scholarship in America, was outstanding for the visitors, and he deservedly bagged himself a goal. The opener had arrived after just three minutes the last time the sides met at this venue, but despite having to wait until five minutes before half-time in this match, Stirling's low finish was delivered with relish after exchanging a neat one-two with Paul Quinn on the edge of the box. Rangers had defeated the might of HMRC (albeit they planned to appeal), and won another heavy-weight battle by keeping their titles, but were struggling to overcome little East Stirlingshire on their own patch.

To be fair, the home side emerged for the second half

with a renewed vigour, but the notable increase in tempo after the restart apparently had nothing to do with an inspirational team talk from the manager, who must have struggled just to be heard above all the bickering from his players.

"The boys were having a wee go at each other at half-time, which was needed," admitted McCulloch. "We knew it wasn't good enough. After having a chat with each other, it showed in the second half, when we came out to play some good stuff at times."

The tough talking worked, and Rangers were back on level terms five minutes into the second period when Little bundled home from close range after reacting to Anestis Argyriou's mis-hit cross. The leveller arrived in time to allow supporters to participate in a pre-planned celebration with extra gusto, as they marked retaining their past honours on the 54th minute by staging a massive "bouncy" in the four stands. There was further reason to celebrate after an hour, when McCulloch latched onto David Templeton's through ball and calmly rounded goalkeeper Grant Hay. The strike took the skipper's tally for the season to twenty-three goals. Not to be outdone, Little claimed his twenty-fourth of the campaign a minute later. The Shire defence stood off the Northern Irishman and his weak shot went under the body of Hay and nestled in the back of the net.

Little had netted his first ever hat-trick in the 5–1 win over East Stirling earlier in the season and still kept the match ball in his living room. The striker and Jimmy Smith were the only players to claim a treble in this fixture, stretching back over six previous league meetings between the two clubs. Little was forced to settle for a double this time but at least remained ahead of McCulloch in the scoring charts. Perhaps the most pleasing aspect of the day's work though was emerging as comfortable victors in the end against yet another side participating in their very own cup final against the Glasgow giants.

Little told me, "It's been a real journey and full of new experiences this season. Things you're not used to are always a bit harder. In the SPL, you've been to all the grounds, you know all the players, you know all the teams and it's just another Saturday. This year, it's been different players and different places in Scotland that you've never been to. I think the most difficult thing this season is playing thirty-six cup finals.

"You get used to that at Rangers, where every team is desperate to beat you, and you expect that. But it's been a different level this season. It matters so much to these players. It's maybe the biggest game of their lives coming to Ibrox and they're all trying to make a name for themselves. I think that's why it's been so difficult.

"It's been great for us. Sometimes we haven't played to the level that we should do, but it's a learning curve. It doesn't matter who you come up against, you've always got to work hard. There is a notice up in our physio's room that says, 'Hard work beats talent when talent doesn't work hard!' and that's been the way we've seen it this year. If you're not prepared to work, you're not going to win these games."

Funnily enough, the SPL commission's verdict arrived fifty-four weeks after Rangers were forced to call in the administrators, but not everybody welcomed the out-come. Celtic – aiming to bring their own tally of titles to 44 this term – declared their surprise at the official conclusion that Rangers gained no competitive advantage from years of making undisclosed payments to players.

A Hoops statement read: "We note the decision that Rangers FC has been found guilty of contravening the SPL rules on disclosure of payments over eleven years between 2000-2011. The scale of this amounts to a deliberate non-disclosure of £47 million in payments to players and staff. We also note the penalty of £250,000 which has been imposed. Like many within Scottish football, including supporters and other observers, we are surprised by the parallel conclusion that no competitive advantage was gained from these arrangements.

"However, the implications of this verdict are for the Scottish football authorities to address since the rules breached were specifically intended to defend 'sporting integrity'. Throughout this matter, Celtic has refrained from comment on the affairs of Rangers FC while the various tribunals and commissions went about their work. We will continue to concentrate on our own affairs and assure our supporters that at all times we will operate within both the rules of our governing bodies and the law of the land."

Speaking after the visit of the Shire, McCoist was unconcerned by the response of their Old Firm rivals, stating, "I was neither surprised nor disappointed, to be honest with you. It went to a commission with Lord Nimmo Smith and two very prominent QCs. You would have to say that's what Lord Nimmo Smith does for a living, make decisions. I'd have to say he's very good at it. So I would rather take his decision than anybody else's, so we are delighted."

Two days later, interim financial results showed Rangers had posted losses of £7 million for the last seven months of 2012. The good news was the amount of cash in the bank at the turn of the year sat at £21.2 million after raising £22.2 million from the listing on the London Stock Exchange in December. The figures illustrated the finances since Charles Green's consortium purchased the business and assets of Rangers after the 'oldco' was consigned to liquidation the previous summer. According to Green, Rangers could "look to the future with confidence and pride".

The chief executive may have been satisfied with how the off-field affairs were shaping up, but he wasn't crazy about the players tasked with doing the job on the pitch.

MARCH 9, 2013
RANGERS 1   ANNAN ATHLETIC 2
Ibrox

Green, the self-styled "outspoken Yorkshireman", will tell anyone who listens that he isn't afraid to call a spade a spade. And he clearly had no qualms about saying what he really thought about the squad at the manager's disposal either. Forget simply the best. Green's own assessment of the current crop of players was rather less complimentary when he labelled them the worst team in the club's history. The Ibrox chief was actually trying to defend the work being done by McCoist when he made the comment in a radio interview, but the message was loud and clear all the same: he simply didn't think the class of 2013 were up to scratch compared to others who had pulled on the famous light blue jersey before them. The visit of Annan was their chance to prove him wrong.

There were no problems with the team bus this time as Annan fronted up at Ibrox with a new manager in tow. Jim Chapman was the third boss – following Harry Cairney and Euan Brydson – to take charge of team affairs for Annan against Rangers this season. He had failed to secure victory in his first seven games in charge and was aiming for a famous win in Glasgow to kick-start his tenure.

In the first half, facing a biting wind, the home side failed to convince or warm their fans before being dealt a major blow, when Dean Shiels was carried off with a knee injury. He was replaced by Barrie McKay wide on the left, with the attacking midfielder later given little hope of playing again this season.

There was worse to come in the second half. With two minutes played, Ally Love handed the visitors the advantage when he met Daniel Orsi's cross and sent a cheeky back-heel effort into the back of the net. Francisco Sandaza replaced Kal Naismith as Rangers chased the equaliser, but the Galabank side incredibly doubled their lead after 55 minutes. David Murray (no, not that one) sent a deep cross to the far post and David Hopkirk bravely dived to head the ball low beyond Alexander.

With the scathing words of their chief executive ringing in their ears, Rangers attempted to stage a comeback and managed to reduce their arrears four minutes later. McKay floated in the corner and, although Sandaza's shot was heading towards a packed goal, Little headed it over the line. Plenty of pressure followed, but Rangers' players did not do enough to contradict Green's withering "worst team" claim as they slumped to their first Division Three defeat at Ibrox.

There were boos from those home supporters who bothered to hang around long enough to hear the final whistle, with pelters directed at McCoist and his players. Over in the corner of the stadium which housed the visiting fans, there was euphoria as Chapman led his team in celebration in front of the away support.

"Ibrox is a fantastic arena, and when I looked at the scoreboard and we were leading 2–0 I had to control myself," said Chapman. "I was telling the players to keep their emotions in check, but I had to control my own emotions. It's my first win, and there are not many teams, at any level, who will come to Ibrox and win."

It is no slight on the efforts and commitment shown by Annan to describe the result as one of the most humiliating in Rangers' history. There could be no excuses about the playing surface or the surroundings, or the unfamiliar style of play in the bottom tier this time – mitigating circumstances which may have been accepted earlier in the campaign as McCoist's men journeyed to unknown outposts while trying to find their way amid a bizarre set of circumstances.

Annan had lost four out of their previous five matches and their most recent away encounter had ended with a crushing 5–1 defeat at Montrose. The victory at Ibrox was only their second on the road since April 2012, the previous win coming courtesy of Clyde at Broadwood in January. And yet, the historic three points gleaned from Rangers in Glasgow did not come as a surprise to chairman Henry McClelland or his coaching staff.

"Queen of the South did it in the Ramsdens Cup on penalties after extra-time, but we were the first SFL team to do it in ninety minutes at Ibrox," the colourful Annan chief stated proudly.

"We are part-time, we train on a Tuesday and a Thursday night, and I always meet with the manager before and after training. On the Thursday evening after training, we were sitting having a chat, the manager, myself, Joycy [assistant boss John Joyce] and the club secretary. We were talking about Saturday's game and how we were looking forward to it. Although Jim Chapman has been in the game for a while, he had never managed at Ibrox. We all just looked at each other and knew we had a chance. We agreed that we thought we were going to do it. We had some kind of feeling that we were going to go there and do well.

"We were in the Blue Room at Ibrox before the game and we were talking to some people in hospitality. They were asking what the score would be and I was having them on, saying, 'Ach, it will be four or five to Rangers.' They said, 'You don't mean that, do you?' and I said, 'No, I bloody well don't mean it. We will win 1–0 or 2–1. I believe we can win.' Well, when we went 2–0 up, it didn't come as a shock, with the way we had been playing. We were winning a lot of the battles and deserved to take the lead and eventually win 2–1."

What followed was a long night of celebrations, with

plenty of paracetamol and Irn-Bru required to ease the hangovers the next day.

McClelland added, "I came home from Glasgow on one of the supporters' buses; I had already booked two seats for myself and my son. We got the bus at half past six and it's an hour's journey to get to Annan, but we got home at 10pm after stopping off for some more aperitifs in Lockerbie. Everybody was as high as a kite. Not high as a kite on drugs, but high on adrenalin and alcohol! We got back into our own social club later on and ended up down the main street on the Saturday night. Of course, it was sore head time on the Sunday, but it was well worth it."

Growing up as a Rangers fan, McClelland confessed he never thought he would see the day when he revelled in a defeat for the Light Blues at Ibrox. He said, "In the lower leagues – and I don't know how many will admit this – but most have their local side and also a 'big' team, boyhood heroes, as well. I supported Rangers and I've always looked for the Rangers results. I supported Rangers particularly in my teenage years. I went to the home and away games, and then I got involved with Annan in the late '70s. Although I've probably seen Rangers hundreds of times, I'll have seen Annan a lot more than that.

"It was really strange to be at Ibrox, seeing Rangers getting beat and cheering when they were getting beat. Before this season, I would never have anticipated the scenario where both my teams were on the park at the same time, although it was always the dream that we would do well in the Scottish Cup and draw Rangers at

Ibrox. It came true, but not in the way we thought it would. We've ended up there twice and on one of the occasions beat Rangers. It was so surreal going through those emotions but it felt great celebrating victory at the place where you've watched your other team. It didn't feel bad at all celebrating the victory. For everybody involved at the club, we will all talk about this day in the future – the day we went to Ibrox and won. For lots of clubs, those days are few and far between, and there will be plenty who have experienced only defeat. Our guys have achieved a bit of history for themselves and the club and they'll be able to live with that forever."

After forty minutes in the dressing room, McCoist emerged to say, "It was a really, really poor ninety minutes. The players know what is expected of them at this club and they dropped below those standards. I didn't have harsh words with them in the dressing room, I just told them that it was unacceptable."

As far as Hopkirk was concerned, the reason for Annan's success over their illustrious rivals was simple, stating, "We just wanted it more." The striker then took to Twitter, along with some of his team-mates, to savour the win and thank their fans. He told his followers, "Still on cloud nine – what a weekend – body is in bits." Fellow scorer Love tweeted, "Thanks for the messages folks! Absolutely buzzing. Great performance from the lads. Cmon!!! Annan fans a big thank you!! #3points #goals." And defender Martin McNiff added, "It was awesome ... got massive respect for Gers fans clapping us off at the end, unbelievable."

Unfortunately for Kyle Hutton, his own tweet did not

go down too well with some members of the Rangers support when he revealed, "Off home to finish off home-land nearly finished the 1st season highly recommend it brilliant watch #twistsandturns." The problem was not his taste in television shows or that he was well behind everyone else who had already watched season two of the popular CIA drama. The problem was the timing of the tweet, at lunchtime a couple of days after the Annan capitulation, when some disgruntled fans clearly felt Hutton and the rest of the team should have been putting in extra hours on the training field instead of watching DVDs. Some even suggested a return to the infamous Jock Wallace days, when gruelling pre-season workouts on the sand dunes at Gullane worked the players so hard some of them ended up vomiting. The players would have been relieved to hear that McCoist was satisfied with the training methods already in place and wasn't planning any trips to the beaches at East Lothian. But they were well aware of the demands to show a major improvement in their next match at Elgin.

MARCH 16, 2013
ELGIN CITY 0   RANGERS 1
Borough Briggs

With four meetings having taken place between the two sides already this season, Rangers were by now pretty familiar with Elgin City. But what about the place itself? Elgin is Scotland's smallest city and lies on the south coast of the Moray Firth, straddling the River Lossie. It has been home to Elgin Cathedral since 1224, and although the Lantern of the North is an historic ruin these days, it's still a fairly impressive place to visit. Elgin is also the birthplace of Elvis. But before fans of 'the King' start flocking to the north of Scotland, I am, of course, referring to the former Rangers and Hearts defender Steven Pressley rather than the iconic crooner.

Elgin City was formed in 1893 when Elgin Rovers and Vale of Lossie amalgamated to form a new football club. They were members of the Highland Football League from 1895 until being granted membership of the Scottish Football League in 2000. City have played at Borough Briggs since 1921 when the ground replaced their Cooper Park home. For fans of Charlie Parker or Miles Davis, the Moray Jazz Club meets at the ground on Thursday evenings in the snooker room on the ground floor. As for Rangers, would they be on song against Elgin, or would they be singing the blues all the way back to Glasgow? Either way, piper Garey Stewart was back to play the teams onto the pitch and entertain the 3,663 fans.

McCoist made four changes to the side that lost to Annan. Hutton was suspended, meaning he had the afternoon free to catch up on *Homeland* or practise some free-kicks, while Shiels was set for a lengthy spell on the sidelines with the knee injury sustained in the last match. Argyriou and Naismith dropped out of the manager's plans, with Sandaza, Sébastien Faure, Robbie Crawford and Fraser Aird added to the side. Faure started in a holding midfield role, with Sandaza tasked with leading the line. The Spaniard went close early on, along with Crawford, but both spurned their chances. Little had become the first player since Peter Løvenkrands to score in six games in a row, but he too was thwarted in the opening exchanges. The vigour with which Rangers launched themselves into the match gradually began to peter out as they ran out of ideas. The decisive goal eventually came in the 72nd minute when referee David Somers ruled that Lee Wallace was impeded in the box by a combination of Sean Crighton and Jamie Duff. McCulloch – despite shoring up the defence – was on target once again when he sent goalkeeper Joe Malin the wrong way from the penalty spot. Rangers had the advantage in terms of goals, but their numbers were reduced when Ian Black was dismissed with three minutes to go for a foul on substitute Gavin Morrison.

"I put my hands up to the first booking," admitted Black. "It was silly and there was no need for it. With the second one, if the referee goes back and has a look at it, he'll be a bit embarrassed with himself. It's a contact sport; there was no kicking, it was just shoulder-to-shoulder. I managed to stand strong and he went down. Sometimes I think the referees are a bit harsh, but I've just got to get on with it."

McCoist described the sending-off as "extremely harsh" but opposite number Ross Jack denied Black was singled out for special treatment by his players, asking, "Why would we target him? He's a good player but he's not a genius. He's not someone that we would set our game plan to stop. No one goes out to harm him."

Celtic defender Charlie Mulgrew had recently confessed he would welcome the prospect of seeing Rangers back in the SPL. Well, sort of. When asked if he would have their Old Firm rivals in the top flight again, he replied, "If it was my choice? Probably, yes." The statement was perhaps lacking in enthusiasm but the sentiment was still there. However, right now, Rangers were struggling to overcome Third Division opposition and McCoist admitted the victory over Elgin was a struggle. He said, "I thought it was a really hard-fought game, as we expected it to be, but we deserved the three points. Hopefully we can get the job done now as soon as possible. It's been a tough old season and a bumpy road, but all we said at the start of the season with this group of players was that we wanted the opportunity to win promotion and win the league. We've given ourselves an incredible chance to do that now."

With resources already stretched, McCoist also revealed his numbers had been depleted further by the decision to release Kevin Kyle from his contract. The big striker had been out of action since suffering injury against Montrose on December 15 – after netting what turned out to be his final goal for Rangers. The former Sunderland and Hearts player found the back of the net three times in thirteen appearances but fell just two games short of picking up a Third Division winners' medal that his former Ibrox team-mates would no doubt be collecting at the end of the season. McCoist paid tribute to Kyle and backed him to do a job elsewhere once fully fit again.

He said, "Kevin has left the club by mutual consent and his contract has been terminated. He goes with our best wishes for the future. He obviously got an injury at a very bad time for him and the club, as he was just getting back in the team and scoring one or two goals.

He'll certainly be fit for the start of next season at a new club. I sat down with Kevin and told him that next season the club would be going in a different direction and we thanked him and wished him well. He was absolutely fine. The big fella has been in the game for long enough to understand and he's a great lad. I've got no doubt Kevin Kyle will be playing football somewhere next season and scoring goals."

With another rendezvous with bogey team Stirling Albion just around the corner, the last thing McCoist needed was to see his attacking options reduced even further. Unfortunately for the manager, that was exactly what was about to happen – and in very odd circumstances.

MARCH 23, 2013
RANGERS 0   STIRLING ALBION 0
Ibrox

Whenever he looks back on the unfortunate incident, Francisco Sandaza will no doubt wish the phone call was actually an automated message about mis-sold Payment Protection Insurance or a cold caller trying to sell him double-glazing or a new kitchen. Or that he hadn't bothered answering the call at all. Instead, the Spaniard found himself participating in a twenty-three-minute conversation with a prankster posing as a Los Angeles-based agent. Using the alias "Jack McGonagle", the hoaxer told the striker he wanted to sound him out about a potential lucrative move to Major League Soccer in the United States. Sandaza allegedly went on to reveal details of his salary and discussed his future plans with the caller, who was actually a Celtic-supporting taxi driver from Glasgow. The man was apparently a known hoaxer who also reportedly duped former Rangers owner Craig Whyte. The conversation with Sandaza was broadcast online and he was suspended by the club and told to keep his distance from Ibrox and Murray Park while they investigated the matter. There was no offer of a dream move across the Atlantic, but the player had inadvertently taken the first step towards an early Ibrox exit.

In a statement, the club confirmed, "Francisco Sandaza has been suspended by the club pending an investigation into comments made by the player in a recorded telephone conversation. The club, Francisco and his agent have had discussions, and manager Ally McCoist also spoke with the player, who did not take part in today's training session. Francisco will not return to the club while the investigation is under way. Rangers regard this as an extremely serious issue but there will be no further comment until the inquiry, which could take a week, has been completed."

Speaking as his side prepared for the visit of Stirling the following day, McCoist added, "Fran has been suspended by the club on full wages pending an internal inquiry. We are very hopeful that the inquiry won't last any more than a week, but he has been suspended and won't be coming to Ibrox or Murray Park pending the investigation. We will be issuing a statement after the investigation. We will have more to say then. I can't say anything that would be to the detriment of the investigation. It is the last thing we need at this moment in time, as we have seven players out tomorrow."

When asked if Sandaza could be sacked, McCoist replied, "I have no idea. We will have to wait to see what the investigation unfolds."

The former Dundee United and St Johnstone striker arrived at Ibrox in the summer as a free agent on the back of an impressive campaign at McDiarmid Park which saw him find the back of the net eighteen times in thirty-four appearances. A season tempered by injury and poor form meant his goal return was not quite so impressive at Rangers, with just two goals from eighteen outings. Even so, a sheer lack of resources meant Sandaza would have been a certain starter against Stirling had such unusual circumstances not dictated otherwise.

With Black suspended for more conventional reasons, Little on international duty with Northern Ireland and Templeton one of a number of players filling up the treatment room, McCoist had no option but to put his faith in the inexperience of youth. Little's absence was all the more exasperating for the manager after the prolific striker found himself stranded in Belfast without a match after the World Cup qualifier against Russia was postponed due to heavy snow. With similar weather in Dumfries and Galloway, second-placed Queen's Park's game at Annan also failed to go ahead, meaning Rangers would have to wait at least another week before having the opportunity to wrap up the title, regardless of the outcome against the Binos. Hutton returned from his ban and was added to the side along with McKay, while Kane Hemmings was handed the number 9 jersey as the lone frontman in what was his first senior start for Rangers. The Englishman had recently returned from a brief but successful loan spell at Cowdenbeath, where he scored four goals in as many games in the First Division. He was now tasked with having a similar impact two tiers below that level.

McCoist admitted, "We spent Friday morning looking at our youth players, not because they deserved an opportunity, but because we needed to fill a jersey. We are in desperate need of bodies."

Fans who braved the sub-zero temperatures were treated to a display of sublime skill and wonderful talent, football of the highest standard to enthral the masses. Unfortunately, the action was taking place on the big screens rather than on the park, as Rangers paid tribute to Davie Cooper with a montage of the highlights of his glittering career, eighteen years to the day after his untimely death at the age of thirty-nine. The former winger had suffered a brain haemorrhage while filming a football skills programme with Charlie Nicholas and sadly never recovered, passing away the following day.

It's safe to say that what followed in this dire match would never make it onto a show-reel of any player's best bits. Three former managers – Walter Smith, Alex McLeish and Davie White – must have been shaking their heads in dismay at what was served up on the pitch as they watched from the directors' box.

Rangers' threat in front of goal was sporadic, their two best chances coming in the first quarter. Lee Wallace played a one-two with Hemmings that put him clean through, but Stirling goalkeeper Sam Filler made himself big enough to block the left-back's attempt to dink the ball home. Hemmings then spurned a good chance of his own when he headed over McKay's cross from the right, before also dragging a shot wide just before the half-hour mark. Stirling should have been ahead by the interval after creating two excellent chances. Jordan White had a free header following Scott Davidson's corner and glanced the ball towards the far corner. Alexander was beaten but Fraser Aird headed off the line to keep the score level. Davidson then found himself in yards of space unmarked at the back post, but Alexander raced off his line and did enough to subdue the midfielder, who blazed his shot over.

The home fans, not for the first time this season, voiced their discontent as the players left the pitch at half-time, but there was no notable improvement after the restart. McCoist brought on Kal Naismith for McKay and switched to a 4-4-2 formation as Rangers battled vainly to break down the resistance of their visitors. Robbie Crawford set up Hemmings, but the young forward was closely marked and once again was off-target as he side-footed wide. It was as good as it got in the second period and it was just as well the champagne was on ice anyway, because this performance lacked the required fizz to secure the win. The final whistle was accompanied by more boos, while the section of the stadium housing the Union Bears displayed a banner declaring, "Less Time Tweeting, More Time Training". Hopefully the twists and turns in the *Homeland* plot had been sufficiently entertaining to justify the continuing aggravation for Hutton following his DVD revelations.

McCoist defended his players, putting the ponderous performance down to the strain caused by a lack of personnel rather than the preparation for their games. He said, "I told you at the start of the season we needed players and I'm not going to change my tune on that. I'll probably go down in history as the only Rangers manager who has struggled to fill a bench. I'm not sure too many Rangers managers have had that problem. But that is where we are.

"If we are going to take a positive, which I always will look for as well, we have had a couple of clean sheets. But in terms of creating chances and taking chances, we are miles short of where we want to be.

"We just have to get over the line. We have to win the title, which is what we set out to do at the start of the year, and then we have to get a team that will win the next title, albeit we don't know what title it will be. It's not rocket science; you look at our squad and we are in desperate need of bodies."

Young midfielder Crawford refused to use youth as an excuse for the below-par display. The twenty-year-old said, "I totally understand the fans' frustration and we all feel it as well. It hurts us just as much and the fans have the right to voice their opinion. They have stuck by us before and we need to do better for them. There was a lot of youth and not much experience there, but we have all come through the youths together so we should know each other's game and we expect to play better than we did."

Responding to the banner in the crowd, another young player, Fraser Aird, assured supporters that the players were putting in plenty of graft in the build-up to matches. He said, "The boys do work hard at training.

We get one day off a week and when we're in we try our best, so it's nothing to do with that. It's about performing better on a match day. The aim at the start of the season was to win the league so getting over the line is the most important thing."

To do so the following week, Rangers would need Queen's Park to slip up at home to Elgin City three hours after their own early kick-off at Montrose.

Aird added, "The Rangers fans are the best but they want to see the team perform well so we've got to work hard and put on a show at Links Park."

MARCH 30, 2013
MONTROSE 0   RANGERS 0
Links Park

Despite their recent poor form, the countdown to another Rangers title was definitely under way, but for Jeff Stelling the fact that the Glasgow giants even found themselves in the Third Division in the first place was a conundrum he still struggled to make sense of. As the presenter of Sky Sports' *Gillette Soccer Saturday* show, Stelling is legendary for his quick-fire delivery of the latest scores and goal flashes, but he confessed that Rangers' unlikely fall from grace took some time to get to grips with. "I have to admit, it has taken me an awful long time to get used to," said the former *Countdown* host.

"Goal flashes will come in and time and again I find myself looking at the SPL instead of the Third Division. Now, in the job I do that is not ideal. And without any disrespect to Berwick, Peterhead and the rest, it does certainly feel unusual reading out their names in games against Rangers. I'm not sure I ever imagined I would be asking the guys for their reaction to an Annan victory at Ibrox. It has been a strange season."

The bad news for Rangers was that a second goalless encounter in a row was on the cards at Montrose. The good news for Stelling was that he didn't have to worry about any goal flashes from the clash at Links Park.

Rangers were handed a tough match the last time they visited the Angus venue in December, leaving with a hard-fought 4–2 win and an apology after the Montrose programme branded the visitors as "the now defunct Glasgow Rangers". This time, the club's official publication appeared determined to make amends, describing Rangers' presence in the bottom tier as "fantastic" for the other nine clubs, as well as stating, "Unlike today's visitors, we don't have a trophy cabinet creaking under the weight of numerous trophies." Whether the Light Blues would be securing another piece of silverware to add to the haul before the day was out remained to be seen.

Perhaps sensing that this meeting might struggle to emulate the six-goal thriller served up on Rangers' last visit to Links Park, there was no sign of any onlookers clambering onto rooftops with deck chairs this time. And they didn't miss much.

Templeton and Black returned from injury and suspension respectively to claim their starting slots on the team sheet, while McKay and Aird were forced to settle for a place among the substitutes. Hemmings was again given the job of leading the line, while McCulloch bolstered the rearguard. Montrose had shipped six goals to Peterhead in their last home match but never looked like suffering the same fate against a Gers attack, with less spark than a damp box of matches and less bite than the statue of Bamse the Norwegian Sea Dog down by the harbour.

"Come on, McCoist. Play a 4-4-2," was the tactical advice from the terraces, as frustrated fans begged the manager to provide a partner for luckless lone striker Hemmings.

"With the greatest of respect to Kane, we don't really have a centre-forward on our books at the moment who can play," explained McCoist, who had recently revealed that Dundee United captain Jon Daly was one of a number of players on his wanted list for next season.

"I can hear people shouting, 'Play a 4-4-2,' but if you've not got two centre-forwards it's very difficult, so you have to try to attack from other areas. We can all see what's happening. There is no real zip or probing or class, actually, in the forward areas, and I think that's evident for everybody to see."

When asked if he thought about moving utility man McCulloch to a forward position, McCoist said, "Of course we did, but we had to balance it out. It would definitely have left us more open at the back; there is no doubt about that. There was the possibility of putting Lee up front, it was an option, but it was an option that we decided not to take."

It was Montrose who should have won the match when a 67th-minute goal by Martin Boyle was disallowed by referee Kevin Clancy for a foul on Alexander – even though television replays showed the goalkeeper was actually nudged by one of his own players, Chris Hegarty. For Rangers, it meant the third match on the bounce without scoring a goal in open play.

Boyle, on loan from Dundee, said, "When I put the ball in the net, I thought it was their defender who hit the goalie. My joy only lasted about three seconds. I didn't ask the ref why he had disallowed it, I just got on with the game. I thought the disallowed goal was a bit harsh so we're very disappointed about that."

Boyle felt that teams were now more willing to have a go against Rangers than they would have been at the start of the season. He added, "I definitely don't think there's anything to fear about Rangers now. Teams definitely turn up believing they can take points from them. That's changed from the start of the season when everyone expected them to have walked the league by now."

Rangers had again left the pitch to the sound of boos from their own fans, but would those jeers become cheers by ten to five?

Myself and a couple of Sunday newspaper correspondents headed for the bar at the nearby Park Hotel to write up as much of our post-match copy as was possible until the result of the Queen's Park game was known. With working Wi-Fi, sandwiches and the BBC football results show on the big screen, we were as well prepared as we could be. Now we just had to wait for the outcome at Hampden.

Twelve minutes into the second half, an excited tweet from the official Elgin City account revealed they had been awarded a penalty. Seconds later, confirmation followed that Stuart Leslie had converted to hand the Black and Whites the lead. Rangers fans demanded more updates from the Elgin Twitter source, but there was not much more to report. Queen's Park failed to respond, the Borough Briggs side held on for the three points and Rangers were confirmed as champions. The spot-kick, given following a collision between the Spiders' Jamie Brough and Paul Millar, was described as "controversial" in the following day's match reports. But Queen's boss Gardner Speirs was magnanimous in defeat, after losing both a game of football and any hope of catching Rangers in the top spot, stating, "Congratulations to Rangers, as they have deserved their title."

It was apt that the championship would be won in such bizarre circumstances in this most surreal of seasons. For a club who had enjoyed so many successes at the national stadium, it was an unusual Hampden victory as they learned of their title triumph while nowhere near the Mount Florida venue. McCoist's men were still on the team bus on the way back to Glasgow when their status as Third Division Champions was confirmed, and so they opted to stop off in Perthshire for a celebratory drink.

The sign outside the Smiddy Haugh Hotel in Aberuthven's Main Street reads: "Sorry! No football coaches or colours!" Thankfully, pub landlord Chris Foulkes relaxed his strict rules when the entire Rangers squad appeared in his bar in their club tracksuits. McCoist is the man whose glass is always half full, and he was finally able to top it up with some celebratory bubbly now that the job was done – while others had to settle for soft drinks as they toasted the success.

"It was hilarious," said the manager. "We stopped off right on the final whistle of the Queen's Park–Elgin game, when we knew we had won the title. As you can imagine, we walked in and some of the lads are still only old enough to drink lemonades. When we got into the pub, there were two punters at the bar and they quickly shouted to the owner of the place to remind him of his strict rules about having no football colours! With twenty Rangers players standing there in their tracksuits, it was very funny and we stopped there for about half an hour for the boys to have a celebratory drink, which was well earned.

"I could sense after the game at Montrose that the reporters thought I should be disappointed with the result and performance, which I probably was. But I finished up by saying that point could win us the league – which it did."

There aren't many teams who are booed off the pitch the day they win the title, and there will be those who will question the lack of finesse as Rangers stumbled over the finish line in unconvincing style. Some will point to the reported £7 million wage bill, the second highest of the forty-two teams in Scotland, while others will counter that factor by stressing this was a squad hastily assembled, with a transfer embargo looming, after just six players turned up for the first day of pre-season.

The history books will report the facts, that the championship was won with five games to spare, with 22 points separating Rangers and their nearest rivals and with just two defeats when the task was completed. The title wasn't in the bag before the Christmas decorations came down – as some predicted at the beginning of this adventure – but it was won before the Easter eggs were scoffed. Only Queen of the South did it quicker, with Celtic the last of the four champions to secure their crown twenty-four hours after Partick Thistle won the First Division. It was McCoist's first piece of silverware since replacing Walter Smith at the helm and the first time in history that both halves of the Old Firm clinched titles in the same season. Some might argue that the most meaningful victories – such as the "Big Tax Case" and retaining all of their previous 54 titles – were won off the pitch, but McCoist was determined to celebrate the club's latest honour as much as he revelled in any of his past achievements with Rangers. He said, "We've been the best side in the league. The fact we are sitting 22 points ahead would indicate we are thoroughly-deserving champions. There's no doubt about that. What a journey it has been. There has never been a dull moment from Elgin to Annan, from Peterhead to Montrose. The hospitality these people have shown us has been first-class. My overriding feeling is of a job well done."

Following a tumultuous summer, when he feared Rangers would be denied the opportunity to play football altogether, McCoist was largely enjoying the lower-league experience. Even if completing a pre-match team talk had proved to be a challenge in itself at times. He said, "We were delighted just to get the chance to play football. I'll always remember Tony Ford of East Stirling at the SFL's meeting at Hampden last summer. I walked in and he stood up and welcomed us and said, 'It's nice to see you.' It was the first time anyone had welcomed us, and I was grateful.

"Then, in the first league game of the season, the Peterhead chairman, Rodger Morrison, chapped the dressing room door two minutes before kick-off to invite us in for steak pie and potatoes after the game. I was giving my team talk and had to bring it to a halt to let their chairman speak!

"I used to believe that we have far too many teams in Scotland. But having been to some of the places this year, it would be complete hypocrisy of me to say there shouldn't be an East Stirling or an Elgin. As long as the clubs can function properly, they deserve to be here."

Meanwhile, several Rangers players took to Twitter to express their feelings about winning the championship. Little tweeted, "Anybody else feel really strange?! Disappointing again today but I suppose we've achieved what we set out to do – may as well enjoy it! #WATP". He then added, "Shows the expectations at the club that we all feel like this! Not good enough but at the end of the day, it was good enough." Hutton told his followers, "Miles harder than it looked winning this title but rewards r sweet as I am finding out right now!!" Naismith was slightly more enthusiastic as he shared his own thoughts: "Yesss!! Not happy about the result but... Glasgowww rangers champions!!! Come onn" Darren Cole, despite his injury woes, was also determined to savour the moment when he tweeted, "Well done to all the boys winning the league ... Wasn't pretty but definitely deserved it #ChampionsRFC"

The final word went to the captain, who already boasted a trio of winners' medals from the SPL but who claimed this triumph topped the lot. McCulloch told the club's website, "There was obvious disappointment after the game, it didn't flow and we didn't play as well as we can. But to hear on the bus that we were champions was the best feeling in the world. I've been lucky enough to win three titles before but I think this is my favourite one. I've been lucky enough to be captain for this one and it means the world to me and my family.

"We can only play against the teams we've been told to play against but, at the end of it, if you are giving me a winner's medal, I am taking it. It really is a dream come true to captain the team and hopefully we can kick on now. This will definitely stay with me for the rest of my life – to captain a Rangers team to win a league means the world to me."

APRIL

Green and Whyte and Grey Areas

APRIL 7, 2013
QUEEN'S PARK 1   RANGERS 4
Hampden Park

Everybody knows the tried and tested formula for your typical Hollywood horror movie. The bruised and bloodied hero or heroine emerges from a near fatal battle, with the villain defeated, and believes they are finally safe from harm. Then, just as they think the worst is over, the dramatic music kicks in and the villain somehow manages to reappear for one final assault on the film's star, often setting the scene for a money-spinning sequel. Rangers must have felt like they were in that movie with the unexpected and unwanted return of Craig Whyte.

The discredited former owner was the man who ultimately brought Rangers to its knees when his failure to pay tax for nine months forced the club to call in the administrators under threat from HMRC. He was the man the fans held responsible for almost destroying their club, the man Sir David Murray claimed duped him into selling his majority shareholding in Rangers for one pound, the man who the Scottish Football Association banned from the Scottish game for life after ruling he was not a fit and proper person to run a football club and the man whose Rangers takeover remained the subject of a police inquiry. Now, incredibly, Whyte was laying claim to the Glasgow giants once again.

Apparently armed with covert recordings of meetings between himself, Charles Green and commercial director Imran Ahmad, Whyte alleged he was involved in their consortium's acquisition of Rangers the previous June and was now demanding £1 million a year for life or 25 per cent of the Ibrox chief executive's shares. Green rubbished suggestions Whyte had any claim on Rangers, its shares or assets, insisting that Ahmad had told the former Light Blues chairman what he wanted to hear in order to secure his shares if needed. The shares later proved irrelevant as an offer to creditors was rejected, resulting in the liquidation of the old company. Always one to find a unique way with words, Green – who denied being a 'front' for the Scots businessman – highlighted his disdain for Whyte by going live on air on *Sky Sports News* and declaring, "Rangers and its fans deserve better than that little google eye."

Speaking ahead of the game against Queen's Park, Ally McCoist admitted he had been unaware of Whyte's claims and would be seeking answers from Green. "It's complete news to me so I'll definitely be meeting Charles and having a chat with him," he said. "Without doubt again, the real people I feel sorry for are the supporters.

The supporters have kept this club going in the last eighteen months, and I definitely feel for them. Just when they seem to be getting a bit of clarity, something else comes out of left field. I would be very hopeful that our supporters can get the answers they deserve."

While Whyte was desperately trying to launch himself back into a starring role at Rangers, those in supporting roles were departing the club. First-team physio Pip Yeates had left after five years of service to focus on his own business, while youth coach Tommy Wilson had quit to take up a new position in America. Joining the exodus was chief scout Neil Murray, who played for Rangers during the 1990s, and who was appointed to the post in 2011. McCoist previously confirmed that his former Ibrox team-mate had been suspended, but Rangers insisted his eventual exit was not the result of any "scandal", adding, "This club has neither suggested nor said anything of the kind. In fact, Rangers are happy to point out that Neil has agreed to act as a consultant for the club."

There was no denying Sandaza had left Rangers under a cloud, though, after being given his jotters by the club following completion of their investigation into the hoax phone call with Tommy the taxi driver.

According to Gers, "Francisco spoke at length to someone posing as an agent and engaged in a conversation which the club believes to be a material breach of his contract of employment. The player was suspended but after careful consideration and a hearing with Francisco and his representatives, the club, and our advisors, believe that dismissal is the appropriate course of action. The termination is subject to the right of appeal under SFL rules and there will be no further comment from Rangers on this issue."

Some questioned whether Sandaza's contract would have been ripped up had he banged in thirty goals this season, but Green claimed even a player as influential as Lionel Messi would have been shown the door had he behaved in the same way. However, Green indicated that he still felt his own players were not even good enough to shine the Barcelona star's boots when he reiterated his "worst Rangers team ever" claim in a newspaper article which hit the streets hours before the meeting with Queen's Park. It had been a hell of a week for McCoist already and there was still the small matter of a football match to be played.

Rangers made two changes following the drab goalless stalemate at Links Park, with Fraser Aird and Anestis Argyriou both added to the starting line-up at Hampden. Chris Hegarty missed out through suspension and Kane Hemmings was dropped to the bench after failing to hit the target as the lone striker in the last two outings. Lee McCulloch returned to a forward role after a spell shoring up defence, with Sébastien Faure taking the skipper's place at centre-half.

Queen's Park showed their class by beaming a congratulatory message on the big screens ahead of kick-off which read: "Congratulations. The President, Committee and all the staff at QPFC congratulate Rangers on winning the SFL Irn-Bru Division 3 Championship." The crowd of 11,492 was down significantly from the 30,117 fans who watched Rangers scrape a narrow 1–0 victory at Hampden in December, but those in attendance were rewarded with a far more convincing display.

David Templeton's opener was the first goal in open play for 318 minutes. Lee Wallace did all the hard work down the left flank before the ball broke for Templeton on the edge of the area and he drove beyond Neil Parry, despite the keeper getting a hand to the shot. This was clearly an arena where Aird flourished, and he doubled the lead by bagging his second goal for Rangers – and his second at the national stadium after claiming the winner against the Spiders earlier in the season. An Ian Black free-kick found McCulloch at the back post and his effort was prevented from crossing the line by the feet of Parry, before Aird reacted to stab home the loose ball from a yard out. Finally, there was some swagger from the newly-crowned champions.

Argyriou appeared to go over on his ankle at the start of the second half and was forced off just before the hour mark, as Hemmings was thrown into the action with McCulloch moving back to defence. The Burton-born hitman handed himself an early birthday present, the day before turning twenty-two, by netting his first senior goal for the club after meeting Templeton's pass and lashing it high into the net with his left foot.

The action was taking place in Mount Florida rather than the Sunshine State, and some of us were still desperately clinging onto the thermals on a chilly afternoon. But the Union Bears decided it was a "taps aff" kind of day and celebrated Hemmings' goal by displaying their bare chests. Thankfully, there was to be no further removal of garments when Barrie McKay was introduced to the action and quickly teed up Templeton for his second of the day, the winger responding with a decent right-foot effort after 86 minutes to wrap up one of the better wins of the season. Queen's Park, at least, avoided the ignominy of being the only Division Three side to fail to score against Rangers, thanks to Lawrence Shankland's back-post header. However, the amateurs joined Clyde and East Stirling as the only clubs that were unable to claim at least a point as a souvenir from their season with the Ibrox side.

When Green first criticised this group of players, McCoist had tried hard to offer a diplomatic response, one that avoided causing disharmony between himself and his boss – or his squad. This time, however, he just about stopped short of challenging the Gers chief – and one-time Frickley Athletic and Goole Town forward – to show him his medals. McCoist launched a passionate defence of his troops and claimed this latest championship – which he had described as "definitely title fifty-five" when I'd put the question of where this honour stood compared to others to him a few days earlier – as the toughest of his own career as player, number two to Walter Smith and boss in his own right.

Deep in the bowels of Hampden, he responded to Green's latest remarks by saying, "It's also the best Rangers team Charles has ever seen, to be honest. Charles is relatively new to Rangers. He knows the job he's got to do, and we've all got to do, and we're looking forward to doing it. In my opinion, it's not the worst Rangers team. I'm not sure how many titles Charles has won in his career, but I've been very fortunate to win fourteen at our football club, including as assistant manager. That title we were all involved in just there is the hardest one.

"I know what it takes to win a title. It doesn't matter what division you are in, it takes a special group of people and talent and hard work to win titles. We've got a group of boys who were assembled in the space of six or seven days and have managed to win a title and they are 24 points clear. I would think everybody could maybe take a wee step back and offer some congratulations to those boys. I'm certainly doing that right now."

McCoist revealed he had held talks with Green in a bid to clarify the situation with regards to Whyte's claims. He said, "I've had a meeting with Charles that lasted for well over an hour. It was absolutely fine; it was absolutely constructive. We are in the same boat – we both want the club to move forward. That's the priority for me and that has never changed. The club must move forward and we are both of the opinion that that's going to be the case."

When asked whether he would provide assurances over Green to wary fans, the response from McCoist was, rather tellingly, not quite as affirmative as it might have been, when he said, "Charles is more than capable of answering those questions himself, to be honest with you. He's never shirked a question and I don't see him doing it now."

Love him or loathe him, there was no doubting that Green had proved himself to be an entertaining, colourful and controversial character during his eleven months in Glasgow, and his comments had generated plenty of debate and talking points on both sides of the border. But another storm was already brewing as a result of his frank and forthright nature, and he would soon add a race row to his collection of front and back-page headlines.

APRIL 10, 2013
RANGERS 2   LINFIELD 0
Ibrox

It wasn't exactly a Bernard Manning stand-up routine in a Northern working men's club in the 1980s, but Green found himself in bother for comments he made about his business associate Ahmad in the same newspaper story in which he had again slated his players.

Speaking in an article in *The Scottish Sun*, Green said, "I was brought up in a mining community where whether someone was black, white, Catholic, Salvation Army, Protestant made no difference. When I played at Worksop Town, the other striker was 'D**kie' Johnson. Now if I say that today I could go to jail. You know, Imran will come into the office regularly and I'll say, 'How's my P**i friend?'"

According to Green, the remarks were actually an attempt, albeit clumsily, to demonstrate that he wasn't a bigot, but landed him in hot water with the SFA, as well as drawing criticism from campaigning group Show Racism the Red Card. The organisation's chief executive Ged Grebby said, "The comments of Charles Green are very ill-advised and someone in his public position should really know better than to use this kind of racist and offensive language. The use of the term 'P**i' is highly offensive and it is something that we at Show Racism the Red Card are trying to educate young people against. For the CEO of Rangers to use the term in any context is not helpful, as it sends out the wrong message to young people.

"Show Racism the Red Card has a long-standing working relationship with Rangers FC. The club is an excellent supporter of our anti-racism and anti-sectarianism campaigns. Show Racism the Red Card work proactively across Scotland educating young people and society about the dangers of racism and sectarianism, empowering anyone who engages with the campaign to become active citizens who safely challenge racism and sectarianism in their own communities and beyond. A significant part of this education is looking into terminology and defining what is appropriate."

Green accused the group of "a knee–jerk reaction" after claiming they had taken his comments out of context, while stressing that he "deplored" racism and sectarianism. He then offered an apology after being hit with a couple of SFA charges, saying, "I apologise unreservedly if any offence has been taken by my remark. I was actually trying to make the point, albeit clumsily, that I am not a racist. Imran Ahmad is a close friend and business associate and I would certainly have no cause or wish to offend him."

As far as close friends go, Irish League champions Linfield were right up there as far as Rangers were concerned. At a time when the Light Blues felt there was a distinct lack of solidarity, camaraderie and general goodwill among their colleagues in the SPL during the club's darkest hour, the Belfast Blues had stepped up to the mark with a genuine offer of help the previous May. With Rangers mired in a financial crisis, Linfield hosted a special fundraising match to help generate much-needed cash. Among those armed with an orange collection bucket for donations was then Rangers striker David Healy's dad, Clifford. While his son was on the Windsor Park pitch helping the visitors to a 2–0 win, thanks to goals from Alejandro Bedoya and Barrie McKay, Healy Snr was urging punters to part with their cash and help save the Glasgow giants. The Rangers survival bid was bolstered when Linfield handed over a cheque for £100,000, raised through gate receipts and donations. Almost twelve months later, the Scots showed their gratitude by inviting Northern Ireland's most successful football club to play at Ibrox for the first time.

Linfield were established in March 1886 by a group of linen millworkers at the Ulster Spinning Company in the Sandy Row area of South Belfast. They have played at Windsor Park since 1905 and opened their 4,200-capacity South Stand in 1930 with the visit of Bill Struth's Rangers in a goalless draw. With the club motto *Audaces Fortuna Juvat*, "fortune favours the brave", David Jeffrey's side boasted 51 Irish League titles – second only in the world rankings to Rangers' 54 championship successes. This was the fifteenth meeting between the two clubs, with Rangers triumphing on twelve occasions. With Stena Line offering a special deal of £65 for a day trip to the game, including a match ticket, around 600 fans made the trip across the Irish Sea for the historic clash.

It took Rangers until three minutes before half-time to find the back of the net when Northern Irish defender Hegarty found the corner of the goal from Aird's deep cross to open his account for the club. McCoist, at fifty years of age, showed he was still down with the kids when he celebrated the goal with some "Gangnam Style" moves, albeit his chances of following Robbie Savage onto *Strictly Come Dancing* remained slim. The visitors had the ball in the net after 65 minutes, but Peter Thompson's effort was ruled offside, before Rangers wrapped up the win with the last kick of the ball when Andrew Murdoch's deflected twenty-five-yard drive deceived Alan Blayney and found its way home. By the end of the ninety minutes, youngsters Alan Smith, Luca Gasparotto, Charlie Telfer, Daniel Stoney and Ryan Sinnamon had all made their senior debuts, with twenty-one-year-old Kal Naismith the oldest Rangers player on the park at the full-time whistle. The match was marred slightly by injury to Argyriou and McKay, the latter's season over with a broken bone in his foot.

Canadian teenager Gasparotto – juggling his football career with studying for his Highers at Bearsden Academy – hoped his outing would pave the way for some competitive action before the season was out. The eighteen-year-old said, "Getting a taste of league action would be terrific. Everyone in my age group knows we're just one step away, so you have to be prepared when it comes. Games like the Linfield one are the perfect way to start, because it was competitive but still a friendly. I thought the best I could have hoped for was fifteen to twenty minutes so to get the entire second half was great, especially at Ibrox. It's been great to see Fraser Aird doing well in the first team and I hope a few others get their chance before the season's over." On the game itself, McCoist said, "It was a thank you for the support Linfield gave us in our hour of need. It was a great occasion."

Earlier in the week, the Rangers boss had defended coaching standards at Ibrox in response to reports that claimed Green had asked him to consider sacking assistant manager Kenny McDowall and first-team coach Ian Durrant. And, like McCoist, who had no intention of allowing recent exits from the Govan club to extend to his trusty lieutenants, Linfield manager Jeffrey also had nothing but praise for the backroom staff. He said, "Linfield's first visit to Ibrox in 127 years is so special, although it has come about through unfortunate circumstances. I've always been welcomed here. Ally, Kenny and Ian are quality people and I would like to congratulate Rangers on their success this season."

APRIL 13, 2013
RANGERS 2   CLYDE 0
Ibrox

Clyde players also acknowledged Rangers' efforts by forming a guard of honour to salute the new champions in their first competitive home match since officially ending the title race as a contest. But the visit of the Bully Wee proved to be little more than a sideshow to the drama which was unfolding off the park over in the leafy suburbs of Milngavie.

Directors of the club were locked in talks in a board meeting at Murray Park, and speculation was rife that

Green's departure could be confirmed before the referee's final whistle at Ibrox as a result of those accusations of duplicitous dealings with Whyte. Others suggested Walter Smith could quit his role as non-executive director amid all the fresh turmoil, just as the previous year's emotional upheavals appeared to be confined to the past. By half-time it became apparent that neither scenario was going to happen – at least not for the time being, anyway – when a statement was handed out to journalists in the media gantry, along with the pies and Bovril, confirming a probe would be launched into the claims instead.

It read: "The board has announced it is to commission an independent examination and report in view of recent allegations in the media concerning the chief executive, Charles Green, the commercial director, Imran Ahmad, and their management of the club. The decision to commission the examination was taken unanimously by those in attendance at today's meeting including non-executive and executive directors. The independent report will be commissioned and completed as speedily as possible and presented directly to the non-executive directors of the company.

"The chief executive will not be involved in the conduct of the examination. The board wishes to make clear that it is not prejudging any of the issues involved and that the object of this exercise is to clarify the situation to the satisfaction of shareholders, supporters, staff and board members. Instructions recently given to lawyers in England and Scotland with a view to taking legal action to challenge these recent allegations will form part of the independent examination."

The board accepted that Green was not a racist after he apologised to directors for his remarks, but they made it clear he was on his own as far as defending himself against the SFA notice of complaint.

The statement concluded: "Mr Green told the board that in trying to make a point in the interview that, as chief executive, he would not countenance any form of prejudice towards employees or players at the club, he had exercised poor judgement in the words he chose. He apologised. The board accepted the explanation that there had been no intention to cause offence and accepted the chief executive's apology.

"The board is satisfied that the chief executive did not act in a racist manner but reminded him of the importance of all office bearers at Rangers upholding the standards expected by the club. Mr Green will deal with the pending SFA charge on this matter on a personal basis. The board wishes to reiterate Rangers is a club which is opposed to all forms of prejudice and has a long-established policy of working extensively in the community through a variety of programmes and initiatives to tackle issues such as racism and sectarianism."

Green, Smith and the other top brass had taken their seats at the game just before kick-off and fans in the singing section, having heard news of the investigation, pointed towards the directors' box and chanted, "Charlie, Charlie, give us the truth." The demands were followed by a chorus of, "We don't care about Charles. He don't care about us. All we care about is Rangers FC."

The Tony Hart Loyal had been getting creative again

before the match and their latest sign declared, "The journey's long, it's only just begun." The accompanying picture of three peaks, increasing in size, and a Rangers flag planted on the smallest mound, suggested a reference to their rise through the leagues. On the basis of recent headlines, it could just as easily have summed up the continuing disquiet behind the scenes.

On the park, Mitchell started the match at right-back in place of the injured Argyriou and performed well enough to earn himself the sponsors' Man of the Match award. Gasparotto was granted his wish when he made his senior competitive debut after replacing the crocked Emílson Cribari at the interval and slotting into the heart of defence. Rangers opened the scoring ten minutes into the second half, when a Templeton ball was met by McCulloch and he lashed his twenty-fifth goal of the season beyond the grasp of Jamie Barclay. The strike meant Jig and Andy Little were the first Rangers strike force to hit fifty goals in a season since their gaffer and Mark Hateley twenty years earlier. There was another maiden bow when Stoney was thrown into the action for Aird with six minutes to go, before Kyle Hutton made sure of the points with a couple of minutes remaining when he dispatched an angled drive past Barclay and into the far bottom corner.

McCoist said, "There were a lot of good positives. Gasparotto came on in the second half and I thought Andy Mitchell was absolutely terrific at right-back. I was delighted with him and delighted for him. Then we brought on sixteen-year-old Daniel Stoney at the end, so it has been a good day.

"The younger boys have got everything to play for – they've got their futures to play for. I would be very hopeful that the standard of football and the level of enthusiasm to play will definitely be there between now and the end of the season."

Mitchell was hoping a couple of fine performances – combined with some bribery to sweeten the deal – would earn him a new contract, and he must have been praying McCoist loved Milk Tray. The defender said, "I have got a few games left and I want to show the gaffer I deserve a contract. I'm still waiting on Rangers getting back to me and hopefully they will do. Put another good performance in to get a new contract is all that has been said. I left a box of chocolates on the gaffer's desk. I want to stay here, everyone knows that. Rangers is where I want to be and I love Ibrox and everything about the club. I will be working hard in the next few games to show I deserve a new deal. I am out of contract next month so I am just waiting on them getting back to me."

Also keen to avoid a summer of uncertainty for very different reasons was McCulloch, who had experienced first-hand the fall-out from the Whyte era, and who admitted, "A bit of clarity would be great. And just the truth. I think everybody deserves to know the truth."

"Green Out Now!" screamed one spray-painted banner in the Copland Road stand during the game, which was angrily torn down by a disgruntled fan, who took exception to the message. It was replaced by another sign, stating, "Alexander Must Stay", a reference to the goalkeeper's on-going wrangle with the club over a new deal and the likelihood that he was set to quit in the summer. But who was likely to depart Ibrox first – Green or the goalie?

APRIL 20, 2013
RANGERS 1   PETERHEAD 2
Ibrox

Just when it appeared that Whyte had no more surprises up his sleeve, he produced another belter. His latest scheme for making money out of the club? Rangers: The Movie. The story had twists and turns, ups and downs and goodies and baddies all right, although coming up with a credible plot might be a challenge even for the best screen-writer in the business when you considered some of the far-fetched and farcical events of the last couple of years. Whyte clearly felt this particular blue movie would have all the elements required to persuade film fans to stock up on the popcorn and flock to their nearest big screens, after it emerged that he had agreed to sell the book and film rights to the story of his takeover and the financial collapse of Rangers.

In an announcement to the Stock Exchange, Worthington Group plc said they had acquired a 26 per cent stake in Law Financial Limited – one of Whyte's companies. According to the group, the assets of the firm included the legal action Whyte had apparently launched against Green. In a statement, the Worthington Group said, "It has also been agreed that, pursuant to the agreement certain other related rights, assets and causes of action will be transferred to the Law Financial Group or directly to Worthington. Those assets include the book, film and television rights to the two takeovers of

The Rangers Football Club in 2011 and 2012 as it relates to Craig Whyte. It is intended that these rights will be commercialised in due course."

So, who would be cast in the key roles in the movie? With his fondness for undercover recording gadgets, Whyte probably fancied the current James Bond, Daniel Craig, to take on his own part, although Christopher McDonald, who played Shooter McGavin in *Happy Gilmore*, was a dead-ringer for the former Gers chief and would be the more sensible casting option. With his previous acting experience, McCoist could play himself but would probably be reluctant to become involved in another Whyte production. The manager's *A Shot at Glory* co-star Robert Duvall might be keen on having another crack at a football flick by playing Green, although, having already struggled with a Scottish accent, taking on the role of a Yorkshireman may be asking too much. There was also the issue of the Oscar-winning actor having his time on screen cut short by Green's real-life resignation and subsequent quick getaway to France.

Green's decision to step down from the position with immediate effect was confirmed by Rangers to the London Stock Exchange just before close of play on the Friday afternoon prior to the visit of Peterhead. Green said, "Recent events have undoubtedly been a distraction for both myself and all involved with Rangers and I feel that it is appropriate that I step down so that the club can continue to progress back to where it belongs at the pinnacle of Scottish football.

"I am very proud to have been associated with a club

of the stature of Rangers and am proud of the achievements of the club during my tenure as chief executive.
My thanks go to the Rangers fans, whose support has
been tremendous during my time at the club."

Rangers added in a statement of their own, "Recent
weeks have seen media interest in the circumstances
surrounding the period prior to the acquisition of the
club by the consortium led by Mr Green. Whilst Mr
Green strenuously denies any wrongdoing, he has
recognised that this negative publicity is a distraction
and is detracting from the achievements and reputation
of the club.

"As a result, Mr Green has informed the board that
he will leave his post with immediate effect and leave the
company, following an orderly handover, by the end of
May. The board has commenced the search for a new
chief executive and expects the role to attract high-
quality candidates from both within and out with the
industry."

By the time the Blue Toon came calling, Craig Mather
was already the hot favourite to land the job. The forty-
two-year-old was a shareholder and had been the club's
director of sports development since October. Mather
invested in Rangers prior to its initial public offering in
2012 and held 3.1 per cent of the Company's shares in
issue. His other business interests included a sports
management firm and a packaging company. A rather
suave-looking individual, with slicked-back black hair
and a tan no doubt topped up by business trips around
the globe, his photograph on Simply Sport Management's
website showed him feeding a baby tiger. Next to the pic,

the company's managing director's biography stated, "Craig blends sharp business acumen with a passion for sport. Football is his main love, having played to semi-pro level and coached in America's A-League. He also runs a successful horse racing business with the assistance of former advisors of Sheikh Mohammed."

Mather sat among the directors in the main stand as Rangers attempted to end another difficult week with a victory on the park. The theme for the day was "The Blue Sea of Ibrox", with blue flags on display in the Broomloan Front, along with a large illustration of a ship, while fans belted out the popular Gers tune with extra enthusiasm. However, the good ship Rangers was again rudderless as the club continued to navigate its way through choppy waters.

The Ibrox side were boosted by the welcome return of Little after a month out of action with a knee injury, while Hegarty was back in the side after serving his ban. Cribari missed out with a knock and Robbie Crawford dropped to the bench. McCulloch's impressive scoring form continued when he fired the home side into the lead with just 12 minutes on the clock after pouncing on a loose ball and lashing his twenty-sixth goal of the season high into the net. The skipper should have added to his tally when Templeton whipped a tempting cross from the right into the box, and McCulloch just failed to connect and stab home. Instead, it was Peterhead who had the net bulging after 23 minutes. Ryan Strachan floated a corner into the goalmouth and Scott Ross reacted first with a back-post header that fell beyond the reach of Alexander.

The woodwork prevented Rangers from restoring their lead when Little cushioned the ball into the path of Templeton, who unleashed a shot that appeared to be goal-bound. The winger wheeled away to celebrate and looked back in disbelief as the effort smacked off the post. Rangers were left ruing missed opportunities when Peterhead surged into the lead after 56 minutes. Rory McAllister collected Steven Noble's pass and rifled into the top corner to claim his tenth goal in six matches.

It was the second home defeat in SFL3 and the eleventh time Rangers had dropped points in the bottom tier. With their all-white strip, Peterhead almost looked like their hosts when attired in their own away kit, and they certainly played more like a team who had just won the championship. But McCoist claimed he would rather focus on rotten results like this one than continue to spend his time discussing off-field issues. He said, "What I want is to come into every press conference and sit here talking about football – about teams, players, bad results and good results. That, for me, would be stability. I never felt we had put it all behind us. I always felt there were things unfolding because there were stories appearing."

McCoist insisted the fans deserved stability and the truth, adding, "My opinion hasn't changed one bit in the respect that the most important thing will always be the club. We must move forward. No matter who is in charge, we need a little bit of stability, there is no doubt about that. We need to look to build for next season. What the club actually needs is to be totally cleansed, to give ourselves an opportunity to move on. Just everything out in the open. And hopefully this investigation will do that so we can get everything out in the open, we can cleanse ourselves, everybody can see what has been going on and everybody can see, hopefully, where we are going to go. We've not had a chance to do that."

Taking in the action at the match was former Notts County, Sheffield United and Queens Park Rangers boss Neil Warnock. He had signed Green for Gainsborough back in the early 1980s but, despite his previous ties with the former chief executive, stressed he was not in Glasgow sniffing out a potential job. Warnock claimed he was simply enjoying a day out at the football as a guest of a friend, while holidaying in Dunoon. On his current relationship with Green, he remarked, "We are not on each other's Christmas card lists."

APRIL 27, 2013
EAST STIRLING 2   RANGERS 4
Ochilview

McCoist's wish for fans to be provided with some clarity took a step closer to being realised when Rangers appointed leading London-based law firm Pinsent Masons to work in conjunction with financial experts from Deloitte. Together they would probe the alleged links between Whyte, Green and his associates, and the role of Sevco 5088, the company at the centre of the dispute at the time of the acquisition.

There was a further attempt to bring stability to the club with the appointment of Mather as interim chief executive, as well as handing him the role of chief operating officer. He would remain in the CEO role until a permanent successor for Green was found, and the

Englishman revealed his CV was already in the hands of the board. He said, "I look forward to starting work immediately and would like to make it clear the chief executive's job is a position I would like to take on permanently." He added, "I am well aware of what this club means to so many people. I have been working at Rangers for the last year or so and the commitment and passion from the supporters never ceases to amaze me. They deserve so much better than they've been getting of late. My job will be to make sure the work is put in to make them even prouder to be Rangers fans. It is incumbent on everyone working for Rangers that we make sure the club is in the best possible shape for next season and to create the platform on which fans can enthusiastically support the team."

Just as Mather was settling into his new office, Ahmad was clearing out his own desk. He had found himself at the centre of newspaper reports suggesting that messages posted under a pseudonym on a fans' website had been linked to the commercial director's official Rangers email account. The online comments apparently accused McCoist and former boss Smith of "trying to take control of the club without putting any money in".

Speaking ahead of the last away game of the season at East Stirling, the Light Blues boss assured fans that himself and his predecessor had nothing but the club's best interests at heart. On the alleged remarks, McCoist said, "I genuinely haven't read them. I'm not really an online person – Facebook and tweeting isn't my forte. But I have been told and kept up to speed with some of the things that have been said. Normally I can't speak for somebody else but I can speak for Walter and I will speak for Walter. The fans can be totally reassured by the fact that all myself and Walter have ever wanted is the best for the club and that will continue to be the case. In no way, shape or form were we trying to take over the club in the last few months. Not at all. All we have attempted to do is the right thing for the club and I can absolutely assure the support that will always be the case."

By the time the match at Ochilview kicked off, Rangers had confirmed Ahmad's departure. Having already stated they would investigate the matter, the club declined to comment on the reasons for his exit.

Wallace was injured, Hegarty missed out through illness and Aird dropped to the bench for the clash with the Shire. Naismith, Crawford and Cribari – who had recovered from a knock – were all given the nod for the final road trip of the season. Reviews of the Brazilian's debut campaign at Rangers had been mixed, to say the least. But despite a tough introduction to the Scottish game, following a more palatable diet of football in both his homeland and Italy's top division, Cribari was keen to remain in Glasgow for the time being rather than take up the offer of a return to his native Brazil just yet. He told *Jornal de Londrina*, "I know the football in Scotland does not have the same prominence as in Italy or Brazil. But I guarantee the history of Rangers is the largest of any club compared with where I have been previously. And to wear their shirt at the age of thirty-three is, for me, a source of great pride. My childhood dream is to return to Brazil and play for Londrina, my first club.

Recently, I met their director, João Severo, in Londrina and he invited me to go train with them. Who knows? It will depend on the situation of the club, my physical condition and motivation. But I still have a year to go at Rangers and will be thirty-four by the time I am finished there."

He added, "Last summer, after I left Cruzeiro, I had three proposals. One to sign for Nautical in Brazil, one for Livorno in Serie B and one for Rangers in Scotland. With the possibility of a new experience at my age, and the greatness of the club, I decided to come to Scotland. Rangers had changed ownership due to bankruptcy and that forced the club to start in the Third Division. I want to get Rangers back to where they deserve to be. They should be in the top division in Scotland and playing in Europe. For me, it is an honour to be a part of this club."

Cribari had already played his part in completing stage one of the process by helping to win the Division Three title. East Stirling, like some of Rangers' other opponents, also paid tribute to the new champions. And as well as a guard of honour, the PA announcer even dusted off an old Queen album for a quick spin of "We Are the Champions" ahead of kick-off for an extra-special touch.

Rangers were ahead six minutes after the first whistle. Little delivered a cross from the right that was begging to be fired into the back of the net and Crawford did the honours with a finish that any centre-forward would have been proud of. The Shire restored parity after 21 minutes when referee Barry Cook awarded a penalty after ruling Kevin Turner was felled by a combination of

Cribari and Mitchell. Paul Quinn duly converted his third penalty against Rangers this season to haul the home side level. But they were dealt a blow on the half-hour mark when Turner was shown a straight red card for a challenge on Black. Commenting on the dismissal, boss John Coughlin said, "Kevin Turner is a Rangers supporter through and through so he is the last person to kick Ian Black. He is more likely to pick him up."

Templeton was on target on the stroke of half-time when he brushed himself off after being fouled just outside the box and sent a superb curling free-kick beyond goalkeeper Grant Hay. East Stirling equalised five minutes after the restart when Quinn connected with a cross from the right and sent a bullet header past Alexander. The visitors managed to edge in front again when Black ran onto Little's pass and dispatched an angled drive into the far bottom corner, before Templeton grabbed his second of the day. Substitute Stoney provided a decent ball across the face of goal, which was missed by McCulloch, and Templeton did well to get on the end of it and fire home at the back post. There was then a competitive debut for youngster Murdoch late on with the points in the bag.

McCoist had jokingly referred to the latest clutch of kids as his "younger, younger players" and Stoney still had the braces on his teeth to prove it. The likes of Stoney and Gasparotto were so new to the scene, the team sheet didn't even manage to get their names right, listing Daniel Sidney and Luca Gaspolito on the bench for Gers. But just like a visit to the bar in *Cheers* (when he was old enough, of course), Stoney hoped fairly soon everybody would know their names. The Rangers rookie said, "This was only my fourth game of the season, including the friendly against Linfield. I was flung on last week against Peterhead, when we were 2–1 down and the fans were shouting at us, but it's been a good experience. The manager has told me to keep doing what I'm doing at my own age group. He tells me to go out and impress him. I was hoping to get into the first team this season and felt if I kept working hard and playing well the gaffer would give me a chance. He has given young players a chance to play and we have hopefully all impressed him. All I have to do is keep doing what I'm doing and hopefully I can get in the side next season."

The Rangers travelling circus was now packed up and preparing to head to pastures new next term and with the decision of Ross County and St Mirren to veto plans for the introduction of the new 12-12-18 league structure for the coming campaign, McCoist's men looked set for promotion to the Second Division after all.

All that was left now was to bring down the curtain on an historic season with the visit of Berwick and the presentation of the Third Division trophy, but the manager confessed his thoughts were already drifting to the summer holidays – albeit his phone was unlikely to be switched off. He said, "I need a break but I won't be getting one right away because there's obviously plenty of work to be done. But I'll get the fishing rod looked out and get away somewhere, that's for sure. You can never totally rest from it though. My phone will be on but where I'm going there are one or two areas where the signal is not great!

"There will be fishing getting done. The family need a break as much as anything and it would be very unfair on them not to go on holiday. I'll be relieved when the season is over – but we are already looking to next season."

MAY

We Are The People

MAY 4, 2013

RANGERS 1   BERWICK RANGERS 0

Ibrox

With a little over twenty-four hours to go until the hand-over of the trophy, I sat down with Ally McCoist in his office at the club's Murray Park training complex to reflect on a season the manager could not possibly have anticipated experiencing when he took the baton from Walter Smith. McCoist is famous for being late, a trait which stretches way back to his playing days when he was, notoriously, always the last one to arrive for training. But remarkably, he was on time for this meeting. It was yet another surprising moment to add to the collection of unusual occurrences that had accumulated over a bizarre campaign. Fresh from the training ground and still wearing his trackies, he looked happy and relaxed. Quite simply, he looked like a man who was relieved that a testing season was finally over with the job done and the mission he had been tasked with at the outset now accomplished. That first game at Brechin City back in July seemed like a long time ago now, but for McCoist, the memory of the sheer relief he felt at just being able to play a game of football was still crystal clear.

He recalled, "We got the licence to play the game on the Friday night and the game was on the Sunday – that's how tight things were. We thought it was great that the game was at least going to go ahead. I can remember pulling into Brechin and the place was pandemonium. The cameras were there and so was the hedge, going all the way along that far touchline. I'd been to Brechin before but the whole thing was just a little bit surreal. I remember at one stage during the game the ball got stuck on top of the hedge. It was surreal and that was the way it was going to be for all the away games in the season. It was the perfect taster for what was ahead of us.

"I knew what to expect at most of the places but I'd never been to Annan and I had never been in the social club at Annan before a game doing the raffle! Getting the biggest cheer of the day after drawing the raffle would give you an indication of the bizarreness of the whole situation, but it was absolutely brilliant. Their chairman, Henry McClelland, made us really welcome and that was an experience.

"He has been fantastic. Just the joy on his face, to see him welcoming Rangers when we went down there, was brilliant. You do realise then just how much it means to these people and their own clubs. There have certainly been one or two characters over the course of this season, and Henry would certainly be right up there challenging at the top of the list.

"He grabbed me out of my team talk because there were a few people he wanted me to meet and a few people to shake hands with, but that's what it's all about. We obviously had to win games of football but we were also making new friends and promoting the club again in the lower division, and I would hope that we have managed to achieve both.

"At Peterhead, I was reminded by their chairman [Rodger Morrison] that there was steak pie and potatoes and Brussels sprouts for my team in the marquee after the game, so the boys went and had their steak pie after that first game of the season.

"There are touches in the lower leagues that the bigger boys could learn from – there is absolutely no doubt about that. They were incredibly hospitable and friendly and it genuinely is just about the ninety minutes for them. When that's done, whether it's a pint of beer in the social club or your steak pie with the Peterhead boys, there are a lot of things the top clubs could learn from them.

"They were great experiences but a real reminder that we were not playing at the top level anymore."

The visit to Forres Mechanics had been one of my own personal highlights of a season on the road with Rangers, and the Scottish Cup second-round tie was also a stand-out experience for McCoist after barely managing to escape from the Moray town with a narrow win and their dignity just about intact.

He added, "Drawing Forres Mechanics in the early stages of the cup was an eye opener. Going up there and reading beforehand that the police had asked local residents not to let fans into their gardens to watch the game was an early warning sign of what we were facing. Forres Mechanics were incredible and, of course, we didn't play well at all but managed to get the 1–0 win thanks to the goal by Kal Naismith."

Steak pies, raffles and hijacked team talks aside, on the whole McCoist reckoned he had pretty much got what he expected as far as the football in the fourth tier was concerned – despite the wild assumptions of some observers.

"There is nothing really that has surprised me," he said. "The standard of opposition has been good and we expected it to be competitive and probably more aggressive than we had been used to, and that proved to be the case. But, I have to add, the quality of the football from some of the opposition teams has been very good as well. We really got what we expected, to be honest. There was a lot of nonsense spoken before the start of the season, with people saying we would go through the season winning every game and all that kind of stuff."

I wondered if now was a good time to tell him about my coupon that had ended up in a bin in Peterhead on the opening day of league business. You know, have a laugh about it now.

"But we felt that was rather disrespectful to the opposition."

Nope, maybe not.

"We certainly didn't believe for a minute that we would do that and that proved to be the case in the first league game, where we got a late equaliser. We knew, to a man, just how difficult it would be and that was certainly the case. You would hope the challenges of this season would stand us in good stead for next season, but it will be equally as difficult for us."

A tumultuous two years at the Ibrox helm meant it was almost impossible to judge McCoist as a manager, having been denied an even playing field during an unprecedented period in the Glasgow giants' history where he found himself as the figurehead desperately trying to hold the club together, as well as putting a team on the park that could win games. But McCoist felt he was now far better equipped to face the challenges that lie ahead, agreeing that his season at the bottom level had made him a better manager.

"Without doubt," he said. "We have had experiences in the Third Division that we are lucky to have had that other managers of top clubs won't get to experience. It's as simple as that. It has certainly broadened my horizons and my experience as a manager, that's for sure. Next year will be the same and hopefully we can continue to progress and I can take all the experiences into hopefully managing at the top level."

With the spectre of administration hanging over the club and months of uncertainty stretching out in front of him, McCoist had pledged his commitment to Rangers with that now famous phrase: "We don't do walking away." Now, fifteen months on and with issues still to be resolved behind the scenes, I asked McCoist if it had all been worth it.

"We will always support the team and we will always be here for the team and the club," he said. "There were times in the last eighteen months where there were serious doubts over whether the club would continue to exist. Knowing how much the club means to thousands and thousands of people, I think we are allowed a little bit of satisfaction and to say a) that we are still playing, and b) we managed to win the league and we have started on the road to recovery.

"The supporters have been unbelievable in terms of their level of commitment to the team. I always hoped that would be the case, but it has been beyond everybody's wildest dreams. Some of the crowds at Ibrox have been absolutely staggering. Every game – Peterhead, Elgin, Annan, Berwick, all over the place – the supporters have been there in their numbers, and I'm really looking forward to thanking them tomorrow, as much as anything, because they have been absolutely brilliant."

McCoist had urged the Ibrox faithful and his players alike to celebrate this championship success as much as they would have revelled in any previous top-flight honour. And with every available ticket snapped up for the final home game of the season a number of days before the event, there was never any danger of a low-key celebration or the occasion turning out to be a damp squib. The red, white and blue bunting was strung outside the pubs on Paisley Road West and fans arrived at Ibrox armed with flags, banners, scarves and balloons. One supporter tweeted before the game: "Which English team will play in front of the biggest crowd in Britain today? Berwick Rangers." He was spot on. Another world record for a bottom tier match was smashed as 50,048 fans crammed into the stadium. The attendance meant Rangers had broken through the 800,000 barrier for the season – and claimed the seventeenth highest average crowds in Europe.

In his programme notes, chairman Malcolm Murray wrote, "Today we will receive the SFL3 trophy and we will all celebrate the end of a season that has seen us return from the brink of extinction." Before the game was even under way, the pitch was flooded with streamers and confetti as players – many with their children – applauded the fans for their support over the course of the campaign.

For the match itself, there was mixed news on the injury front. Lewis Macleod, who had been voted Rangers' Young Player of the Year despite being out of action since January, made his long-awaited return after knee ligament damage to take his place in the team. Defensive problems – Lee Wallace, Emílson Cribari and Chris Hegarty were all sidelined through injury – meant youngster Luca Gasparotto was handed his first senior start after a couple of positive substitute appearances.

Rangers enjoyed the best of the possession early on but struggled to create much in the way of clear-cut opportunities. Aird eventually got the party under way after 32 minutes when he threw himself in front of Kyle Hutton's intelligent cross from the left to send a diving header into the back of the net from six yards. The young Canadian likened the occasion to a Champions League night and he celebrated his goal as though he had just won the World Cup, sinking to his knees and drinking in the acclaim of the crowd.

He said, "It was a brilliant experience playing in front of an absolutely sold-out Ibrox. It felt like a Champions

League night out there. Scoring my first goal at Ibrox means a lot to me, and scoring it on such a big day means even more. My family who are over here were at the game and the rest of my family back home would have been watching it. The Toronto No.1 Supporters Club put on a big breakfast, so I'm sure there were a number of folk over there watching and supporting me, so I'm delighted."

There was a setback for Rangers when Andy Little was forced out of the action five minutes after Aird's goal with a calf problem, but the good news was the appearance of Darren Cole, whose season had thought to be over after ankle surgery. Gasparotto left the pitch on a stretcher right at the end, leaving Rangers to run down the clock with ten men, having used all their subs, but the defender's ailment was nothing more serious than cramp and he was back on the park with the rest of his team-mates in time for the trophy presentation.

Amid all the celebrations, Aird admitted there was one overriding emotion. He said, "It is just a big relief. A big weight has been lifted off our shoulders. We won the league a couple of weeks ago but finally getting the trophy means a lot and those medals mean a lot to the boys. It's the first championship for a lot of us and hopefully there is a lot more to come in the future.

"Hopefully the gaffer does bring in a lot of older boys and experience. It was the experienced boys who took us over the line this year because they have been there and done it – the likes of Lee McCulloch and Neil Alexander. So the older boys he brings in will hopefully just make us better. We want to win the championship again next year so hopefully he brings in enough players and keeps the right balance with the young boys and we can win it again.

"It's been a long journey, to be honest. For us young boys getting a chance this year has been brilliant. I don't think any of us thought at the start of the year that this would have happened to us. It's experience and we've got to take that with us and move on for next year."

Scottish Football League chief executive David Longmuir strode out onto the pitch with the silverware as the team gathered on the blue and orange Irn-Bru podium, with new temporary chief executive Craig Mather savouring the moment in the front row of the rostrum along with the players. Included in the presentation party was Barr's head of financial planning Peter Waddell, the son of the legendary Willie Waddell. To their credit, Berwick players who had sealed a play-off spot despite the defeat and who we hoping to join Rangers in the Second Division next season remained on the park to applaud as the champions were officially crowned.

The big screens flashed up the message: "Thank you, each and every one of you. When all looked lost, Rangers fans saved the day. And because of your unwavering commitment, we have completed Phase 1 of the Journey. Now, with your continued and unprecedented support, we will regain our rightful place. Thank you, we will never forget." Then Tina Turner and the ticker tape were unleashed and Lee McCulloch held the trophy aloft as the place erupted.

"We've turned it around and we've come back," said

former Rangers striker John Macdonald, who had witnessed most games at Ibrox this season as part of his work in the media.

"This is the first step forward. We got the results. A lot of it wasn't pretty, but some of the games were good to watch. Hopefully the young boys will learn from all the experiences they have had this year and will take what they have learned into next year. Lewis Macleod did really well before his injury and Barrie McKay has also done well, so he's another one that I look forward to seeing. It's looking promising for next year."

Like myself, broadcaster Tom Miller had covered much of the country, clocking up the miles with the Light Blues on their travels over the course of the campaign as the voice of RangersTV. He said, "I remember being asked to be on standby the Friday before the game at Brechin because they didn't know if there would even be a game or if RangersTV would be able to cover it. So what chance did the manager have? All I had to do was go there and commentate for ninety minutes or so – Ally McCoist and his backroom staff had to put a team together to compete in a cup against a team who were in a league above them in Division Two. I remember looking at the faces coming off the team bus that day and thinking, 'Goodness, he wouldn't normally be involved' and 'Where has he come from?' and 'Christ, who is that?' They bolted together a team as best they could and they won the match. Everybody left Glebe Park that night thinking, 'At least Rangers are here.'

"Just to get playing was fantastic – then it was a case of uncharted waters in Division Three. It was a case of getting the AA Route Map out and saying, 'So, where is Annan? Peterhead? Do we need to leave the night before? A night out maybe? Okay, that's not so bad!' The start was dodgy. Then, when they got that first win on their travels at Clyde, you could see the cloud lift. The penny dropped and Rangers knew what they had to do to win Division Three."

Lorenzo Amoruso was amongst a host of former stars who were back in Glasgow ahead of a charity Legends match with their Manchester United counterparts. Sitting in the stand with Richard Gough and Arthur Numan, he watched as Rangers lifted a trophy he never thought he would see in their possession. And as much as the Italian defender was pleased to see Rangers add further silverware to the trophy room, he was still saddened by the trauma endured by his old club and their dramatic fall from grace. He told me, "It was emotional, but to have so many players and ex-players here to celebrate a Third Division league title is also a bit sad. Don't get me wrong, it's fantastic when you win trophies, but the whole situation is almost unreal. Let's hope, as soon as possible, that something will be done for Rangers because the fans definitely deserve a better league.

"I think it's the worst dream that any Rangers supporter or any Rangers player could have. It's horrible, honestly. But this is the situation just now and the only thing you can do is just try to win as much as you can, like the team did this season, and see what's going to happen."

Among the medals claimed during his six years as a

player at Ibrox were three SPL championships, and Amoruso added, "Thinking about my own time at Rangers, with the great players who have been here, the whole history of the club is so important and so vital for any Rangers supporter. That history keeps the supporters coming here to every game because, no disrespect, but the football that we are seeing on the pitch isn't really the best. Great memories keep the fans loyal. Hopefully we keep going on and winning leagues."

Having navigated the club safely through stage one of their recovery following liquidation, Amoruso, who played for Rangers between 1997 and 2003, backed McCoist as the right man to guide the club through the Second Division as well.

"He must be," he said. "I don't know how many other managers would have been so patient and who would have understood the level of football. He has been very, very good. People like myself, Ally and many others don't know what it means to play in the Third Division. We probably never even watched a game in the Third Division before this season. No disrespect, but that's the way it was. So it was very frustrating for Ally to organise a team when you probably don't even know the teams you will play against. Ally has done a fantastic job and credit to the young boys as well. He gave them a lot of responsibility and they responded very well. In the end, it was a day for celebration."

Amo's views were echoed by Dutch star Numan, who confessed, "I still find it hard to understand what has actually happened at Rangers. We had so many world-class players at the club when I was there. But I think that when Ally came back last summer he had something like seven players. That's almost impossible to imagine at a club like this. He then had to get a group of players good enough to win the league and win promotion. That's what he's done."

He added, "For a game in the Third Division to get 50,000 for a crowd is unbelievable. It showed what it means to be a Rangers fan. This is only possible at Rangers. I don't think any other club in the world would have had the backing Rangers have had. They are playing in Division Three and yet the fans still come. I often get asked in Holland how it's possible that so many people turn up for games that are played in the bottom division. It was incredible to see so many people here. The supporters have stood by the players, the club, the management – and you have to give them an awful lot of credit."

Little, who finished the season as the club's top goal-scorer in the league, earning him the Sam English Bowl, refused to allow his injury to prevent him from completing a lap of honour.

The striker said, "There have been enough disappointments this season so when a good thing comes along we should enjoy it. It was a really special moment to get the trophy. I'm delighted to be the top scorer in the league – that's massive for me. I will be able to look back in the years ahead and know that I won the Sam English Bowl."

As a player, Little had tried as much as possible to focus on his job on the pitch and generate positive back-page headlines rather than fret over stories about the club on the front pages. An air of uncertainty remained, but the Northern Irishman insisted there would be no excuses for repeating some of the poorer results of this campaign once McCoist's men regrouped for stage two. He said, "All we can affect is what happens on the field and that's where we need to improve by having a good season next time. We haven't been good this season – we have been really, really poor – but we still won the league and you can't argue with that. The front-page stories, instead of the back-page stories, have been a big issue this season and as much as you try to ignore it as a player, it does play on your mind and all the uncertainty is not good. But we start again in the summer and we will have no excuses for underperforming next season. We know the performances have to be better. Whoever we play against next season, the main aim and the expectation is that we will win that league. We had plenty of excuses to make this season if we wanted to. We've no excuses next season."

Rangers had no pre-season to speak of last summer and McCoist was keen on a trip to the United States – a glamour friendly against New York Red Bulls had already been mooted – as well as a training camp in Germany in order to provide his players with the best possible preparation ahead of the new campaign.

Little, who could expect trips to the likes of Gayfield, Somerset Park and Stair Park to follow next term, said, "The aim was to win the league and we have done that, so we will go away now and enjoy a holiday. We have got a big pre-season ahead of us and we will need to concentrate on that."

By the time McCoist arrived in the press room for his

post-match briefing, his suit was already soaked in champagne and nothing was going to remove the smile from his face. Not even questions about a leaked document, which apparently insinuated the removal of McCoist and his coaching staff in favour of top European names. According to reports, the author of this blueprint for the future was believed to be a £1 million club investor named David Gowans. The report, which suggested Rangers should be courting the likes of Johan Cruyff and Frank Rijkaard to oversee the football operation at Ibrox, was apparently penned months earlier but had only just surfaced.

McCoist made light of the situation, saying, "I believe the person who did it was an electrician. If that's the case, I'm heading straight home to do a thesis on the way forward for electrical engineering. Remember, brown is live at all times! If the gentleman who wrote it can get Johan Cruyff and Frank Rijkaard, I can tell you that I will drive over tonight and pick them up and bring them back and they can sit in the office and get on with the job. I would certainly move sideways for those two."

McCoist then went on to speak of his admiration for the club structure in place at Bayern Munich and the importance of men with "blue blood", such as Sandy Jardine, Walter Smith and John Greig, having important roles to play at Ibrox. He paid tribute to players for the job done this term and discussed his hopes that he would prove himself to be the right man for the job the following season.

"I just want the opportunity to do that," he said. "I'll be honest, I don't think there will be massive amounts of change for next season. We will have to get a group of players who are going to get us out of the next division, hopefully with the same margin of points but with one or two better performances."

There was even a mention at the end of the press conference for yours truly, who was promised a glass of wine for being one of the few journalists to make a point of asking him questions about football this season!

By the time he faced a room full of media types, McCoist had already told the fans what they wanted to hear when he took the mic and addressed a packed stadium on the full-time whistle. His voice cracking with emotion and often interrupted by outbursts of cheers and chanting from the stands, he told the sold-out crowd, "It's been an absolutely wonderful occasion. I received a text last night at about quarter past eleven wishing all the staff, all the players and all the supporters congratulations and for us all to have a wonderful day today. That came from Sandy Jardine.

"I also have to tell you, to each and every one of you here today – and who have followed us throughout the season – on behalf of the club, on behalf of the players and on behalf of all the staff, including the management and coaching staff, I would like to take the opportunity to thank you from the bottom of our hearts. Because I tell you something, you guys have shown a support without which this club would not have survived. It's as simple as that.

"We will never, ever go away, that's for sure. The lifeline of our great football club is every one of you in this stadium and every one of you who has shown a quite unbelievable support and love for our football club and that will always continue. With your support along the way, we will get back to where we belong."

McCoist acknowledged that the football on the park had not always been up to the standards expected at Rangers – with the ninety minutes just witnessed falling into that category – but declared himself satisfied with the outcome. He added, "We are all aware that some of the performances haven't been what we wanted. But if you had seen us at the start of the season, six players came in for training and we didn't get a licence to play until forty-eight hours before our first game ... If somebody had offered us the chance to win the title by twenty-odd points, I would have bitten their hand off. It's stage one completed and that's where we are.

"The boys will go away and get a good holiday and what we must do is strengthen the squad, we must look to get some free transfers in. We have to give these lads a hand and we have to bring in as much quality, albeit on free transfers, as we can to launch the attack for next season."

There were still major questions to be answered over what was set to be another long summer of uncertainty. The outcome of the independent examination into the extent of Green's links with Whyte was still to be delivered to the club's directors and there was the need for stability within the boardroom itself with the appointment of a permanent chief executive, whether the position would eventually be occupied by Mather or some other candidate. A huge question mark also hung over Scottish football as a whole, with the subject of league reconstruction still being debated, and with an appetite for some form of change still apparent. Rangers, at least, looked set to be granted the progression to the Second Division, which had, of course, been the number one aim at the beginning of this pilgrimage back to the promised land.

The final word, naturally, went to Rangers manager Ally McCoist, as he reflected on the supporters who had followed them from Forres to Berwick, who snapped up more than 38,000 season tickets within a matter of days and who crammed into Ibrox for every home game, culminating in an astonishing crowd of 50,048 on the final day.

"Quite simply, we are the only club in the world who could do that," said the Light Blues boss before adding, "We are the people."